RAINBOW IN THE MORNING

Edited by
J. FRANK DOBIE

PUBLICATIONS
of the
TEXAS FOLKLORE SOCIETY
NUMBER V
Reprint Edition

FOLKLORE ASSOCIATES INC.
HATBORO, PENNSYLVANIA
1965

MANUFACTURED IN THE UNITED STATES OF AMERICA

CONTENTS

RAINBOW IN THE MORNING

SOME CURRENT FOLK-SONGS OF THE NEGRO

PREFACE TO THE REPRINT EDITION

The fifth volume of the Texas Folklore Society carried only the title of the series. It is now reprinted under a title of its own, RAINBOW IN THE MORNING. Added at the end is the first item published by the Society, a pamphlet by Will H. Thomas on Negro folksongs, which appeared in 1912.

This was the fourth book edited by J. Frank Dobie for the Society. His energy and enthusiasm were stimulating the collection and study of Texas lore. The first printing of *Legends of Texas* in 1924 was rapidly exhausted and a second and larger printing was run off. Readers in general, besides teachers and librarians, were becoming aware that Texas possessed an interesting and valuable folklore.

Dobie's article on the tournament as he knew it in Live Oak County gives information interesting equally to historians of folk festivals and biographers of Dobie. Mary Jourdan Atkinson has recorded many colorful sayings that are seldom heard today. This one calls up a vivid image in a devastating comparison: "I've seen wilder heifers than you milked in a gourd, ma'am." Gates Thomas, Will's brother, has some fine songs that he heard sung by Negro workers in the country around Winchester, where his father had a plantation. His version of the famous "Boll Weevil" song differs somewhat from that collected by Lomax in 1909. Douglas Branch, who had taken a course under Dobie at the University of Texas, is represented by an essay on buffalo lore; at this time *The Cowboy and His Interpreters* had been accepted by Appleton, and Branch later published a book on the buffalo.

It is gratifying that Folklore Associates should bring the present volume back into print, with the addition of Will Thomas's pamphlet.

WILSON M. HUDSON
Secretary and Editor
Texas Folklore Society

Austin, Texas
March 12, 1965

REMARKS NECESSARY AND UNNECESSARY

By the Editor

More and more frequently scraps of folk-lore, newspaper clippings, and book references are being sent in to the Texas Folk-Lore Society. The practice is to be commended. Really, the Society is assembling a mass of raw material.

Some months ago Mr. L. B. Russell, of Comanche, Texas, contributed a voluminous collection of folk tales that his mother had told her children on the Texas frontier three score years ago. Some of them are old English fairy tales; two or three are stories of pioneer life such as mothers tell their children; several of the tales are told in rhyme. It is a remarkable collection. Many of the tales have been in print, but these Texas versions differ materially from printed versions thus far examined. So far as Mr. Russell's mother was concerned, they had never been in print; for her they were an oral inheritance. Then toward the close of her long life when she was between eighty and eighty-five years old she wrote them down just as she had so often told them to her children and grandchildren.

These folk tales are certainly a part of the social history of the state. The Texas Folk-Lore Society considers publishing them next year. With them should be published other folk tales that belong to Texas. Mr. Eddins, of San Antonio, has some delightful Uncle Remus stories of the Brazos bottoms; Miss Louise von Blittersdorf, of Austin, has heard and set down a charming story of Irish fairies in Texas near the old San Gabriel Mission. There are many other charming Irish folk tales peculiar to Texas if only they could be secured. I know a Mexican folk tale or two that might well be included.

This collection ought to be a kind of complement to *Legends of Texas*. It can be made so only by the wide co-operation that made the collection of Texas legends what it is. Everybody who reads this is asked to do what he or she can to make this proposed collection of Texas folk tales representative and interesting.

The editor disclaims any responsibility for the opinions and information set forth by the varying contributors on the subject of negro folk-songs printed in this publication. If one wants to spell negro with a capital *N* and another with a little *n*, the editor has nothing to say; if one considers the negro as a shining apostle of sweetness and light, another as a gentle old darkey, and still another as a "phallic kinky," it is none of the editor's business.

My wife, Bertha McKee Dobie, has aided me in going over all manuscript material, and now she is assuming the burden of reading proof and making an index. My obligation to her is more than I can express.

University of Texas, Austin,
June 11, 1926.

SOME TEXAS VERSIONS OF "THE FROG'S COURTING"
THE WAY OF THE FOLK WITH A SONG

By L. W. Payne, Jr.

I. Introductory Note

One of the most widely known nursery songs in America is "The Frog's Courting," otherwise known as "The Marriage of the Frog and the Mouse." Inasmuch as this song has been in continuous use among Englishmen and Americans for practically four hundred years, as is shown below by actual historical references, a study of the varieties of the forms in which it has appeared within recent times will give the student who is interested in folk songs and ballads an excellent opportunity to survey the methods by which a folk-song is propagated and transformed in its progress from generation to generation. In the following section I have summarized the history of the song from the first known allusions to it in 1549 and 1580, to its first printed musical form in 1611; and through its traditional and stage versions in Great Britain, on down to its importation to America. My principal contribution is found in the last part of the paper in the record of numerous Texas versions which I have collected through the help of my students and colleagues in the University of Texas. I owe thanks to Miss Anne Garrison and Professor Frank L. Reed, both of the University Conservatory of Music, for help in transcribing the tunes of the Texas versions.

II. History of the Song

On the history of the song called "The Frog and the Mouse" a full note, to which acknowledgment of indebtedness is hereby made, is given by Professor G. L. Kittredge in the Tolman-Eddy article, "Traditional Texts and Tunes," *Journal of American Folk-lore*, XXXV, pp. 394-399, Oct.-Dec., 1922. The principal early references to the song are three: (1) The title of a song possibly to be identified with later versions, found in Wedderburn's "The Complaint of Scotland" (1549,

ed. Murray, p. 64) and referred to as "The Frog Cam to the
myl dur"; (2) Stationers' Register (Collier II, 132; Arber II,
382), Nov. 21, 1580, a ballad entitled "A Moste Strange Wed-
dinge of the ffrogge and the Mouse," licensed along with three
other ballads to Edward White (Collier says in a note, "this
can hardly be any other than the still well known comic song
. . . sung in our theatres and streets") ; (3) the oldest extant
version of the song in Thomas Ravenscroft's *Melismata*
(1611), given as No. 21 under the section of "Country Pas-
times," with tune harmonized for four voices. This song was
reprinted by the Roxburghe Club, Part II, 16, in 1822, and
has been frequently reprinted in modernized forms since that
date. As a study of the later tunes must be based on Ravenscroft's music, the tune and words are reproduced here from
a photostat of two pages of the *Melismata*, a copy of which is
in the Library of Congress.

COVNTRY PASTIMES.

¶ The Marriage of the Frogge and the MOVSE.

Treble.   **21.**   **4. Voc.**

'T was the Frogge in the well, Humble-dum, humble-dum. And
the merrie Mouſe in the Mill, tweedle, tweedle twino.

2 *The Frogge would a woing ride,*
   humble dum,humble dum
Sword and buckler by his ſide,
   tweedle,tweedle twino.
3 *When he was vpon his high horſe ſet,*
   humble dum,humble dum
His booss they ſhone as blacke as iet
   tweedle,tweedle twino.
4 *When ſhe came to the merry millpin,*
   humble dum,humble dum
Lady Mouſe beene you within?
   tweedle,tweedle twino.
5 *Then came out the duſty Mouſe,*
   humble dum, humble dum
I am Lady of this houſe,
   tweedle,tweedle twino.
6 *Hiſt thou any mynde of me?*
   humble dum,humble dum
I haue e'ne great minde of thee,
   tweedle,tweedle twino.
7 *Who ſhall this marriage make?*
   humble dum,humble dum,
Our Lord which is the rat,
   tweedle,tweedle twino.

8 *What ſhall we haue to our ſupper?*
   humble dum,humble dum,
Three beanes in a pound of butter,
   tweedle tweedle twino.
9 *When ſupper they were at,*
   humble dum,humble dum
The Frog,the Mouſe,and euen the Rat,
   tweedle,tweedle twino:
10 *Then came in gib our cat,*
   humble dum,humble aum,
And catcht the mouſe euen by the backe,
   tweedle,tweedle twino.
11 *Then did they ſeparate,*
   humble dum,humble dum,
And the frog leapt on the floore ſo flat
   tweedle,tweedle twino.
12 *Then came in Dicke our Drake,*
   humble dum,humble dum,
And drew the frogge euen to the lake,
   tweedle,tweedle twino.
13 *The Rat run vp the wall,*
   humble dum,humble dum.
A goodly company, the diuell goe with all,
   tweedle,tweedle twino.

The traditional versions are numerous. Ritson gave the English traditional version in *Gammer Gurton's Garland* (1810), and Halliwell reprinted this version in *Nursery Rhymes of England* (Percy Society, 1842). This version is closely related to the *Melismata* song, but it has the *Kitty-alone (cf.* Scotch *Cuddy-alone)* burden. It has been frequently reprinted in English nursery or Mother Goose rhymes. Kittredge reports five Scottish traditional versions (see JAFL, *loc. cit. supra)* and several American versions. Mrs. Ella Mary Leather gives a fragmentary text taken down from an Irish nurse *(Folk-Lore of Herefordshire,* 1912, p. 209), and a fuller Irish version is given by a correspondent in *Notes and Queries,* First Series, II, 75 (1850). Since this last is the first traditional version which gives the wedding-guest feature, a common feature of nearly all American versions, it is reprinted here for comparison.

1   Misther frog lived in a well,
    Heigho! my lanti-iddity!
And the merry mouse in the mill,
    Terry heigho! for lang for liddity!

2   Says Misther Frog, "I will go coort;
Saddle me nag and polish me boots."

3   Frog came to Lady Mouse's hall,
Gave a rap and thundering call.

4   "Where is the people of this house?"
"Here I am," says Lady Mouse.

5   "I've come to coort Miss Kitty here,
If that she can fancy me."

6   "Uncle Rat is not at home;
He'll give you an answer—I have none."

7   Uncle Rat when he came in,
"Who's been here since I left home?"

8   "Misther Frog, a worthy man;
Give him a wife, sir, if you can."

9   "Where shall we made the bride's bed?"
"Down below in the horse's head."

10   "What shall we have for the wedding-supper?"
     "A roasted potato and a roll of butter."

11   Supper was laid down to dine,
     Changed a farthing and brought up wine.

12   First come in was a nimble bee,[1]
     With his fiddle on his knee.

13   Next come in was a creeping snail
     With his bag-pipe under his tail.

14   Next came [sic] in was a neighbor's pig,
     "Pray, Good People, will you play us a jig?"

15   Next come in was a neighbor's hen,
     Took the fiddler by the wing.[2]

16   Next came in was the neighbor's duck,
     And swallowed the piper, head and pluck.

17   Next came [sic] in was the neighbor's cat
     Took the young bride by the back.

18   Misther Frog jumped down the well,
     "Zounds, I'll never go coort again."

19   Uncle Rat ran up the wall,
     "Zounds, the Devil's among you all!"

Similar American versions with tunes are given in Wyman and Brockway's *Lonesome Tunes* (Kentucky) and Campbell and Sharp's *English Folk-Songs from the Southern Appalachians.* For further references to these and other American versions see Kittredge's Note, *loc. cit. supra.*

About 1809, John Liston (1776-1846), the English comedian, sang on the comic stage a version with tune by Charles Edward Horn and accompaniment by Thomas Cook. This version introduced certain stage allusions, the opera-hat, beer-drinking, singing a song, and so forth. The song appears to be a stage adaptation of the original version with the *Rowley*

---

[1]Transformed into *bumblebee* in the American versions.

[2]This tragic accident to the bee is probably the source of the otherwise silly ending in several American versions—"So this was the end of one, two, three, The frog, the mouse, and the bumblebee."

Powley burden.[3] It struck the popular fancy and soon replaced
the Ritson-Halliwell nursery rhyme, particularly in the American editions of Mother Goose rhymes. In Davidson and Sur-
ette's *One Hundred and Forty Folk-Songs* [1917?], for example, I find this stage version reproduced and marked "English Folk-Song, Anonymous." Anyone with an ear for folk

---

[3]In *Notes and Queries*, First Series, II, 27 (1850), a correspondent
signing himself "Chethamensis" says a part of the *Rowley Powley* chorus
was used in 1809 at the installation of Lord Grenville as Chancellor at
Oxford. He quotes one stanza as follows:

> 'Mr. Chinnery, then an M.A. of great parts,
>   Sang the praises of Chancellor Grenville.
> Oh, he pleased all the ladies and tickled their hearts;
> But, then, we all know, he's a master of arts,
>   With his Rowley Powley Gammon and Spinach
> Heigho, says Rowley.

Whether this burden was borrowed from Liston's song or whether both
are derived from an earlier traditional burden is uncertain. Other correspondents in *Notes and Queries* give considerable additional material on
the traditional and stage versions. In the May 11th, 1850, number (Vol.
I, p. 458) a correspondent signing the initials R. S. S., answering a query
in a previous issue, says that the *Heigho, says Rowley* chorus was probably not over thirty-five years old when Liston sang an altered version of
the very old song and inserted instead of the older burden his *Heigh-ho,
says Rowley* burden. He also says that in his interleaved copy of Halliwell's *Nursery Rhymes* he had placed the original song of "The Frog
and the Mouse" with three different melodies and nonsense burdens as
sung by his nurse, Betty Hichens. (These versions, so far as I know,
have never been printed.) A second correspondent (initials T. S. D.), a
sexagenarian, in the June 15 issue, says he remembers the jingle from his
earliest childhood, and asserts that it was universally known in the
remote provincial village high up the Severn, and hence was much
older than the previous correspondent had thought. He even surmised
that the song had a politico-religious application, and might refer to
Henry VIII and Anne Boleyn, saying that the "frog" in

> The frog he would a-wooing go,
> Whether his mother would let him or no,

would not inaptly represent the "wide-mouthed, waddling Henry" and
the "mother," the Church, and that the "gleesome Anna would be 'the
merry mouse in the mill.'" In the June 29, 1850, issue (II, 74), the old
song calls forth four notes from different correspondents. One says that
"Old Rowley" was a name familiarly applied to Charles II. Another
calls attention to the Stationers' Register entry, quoting Collier's note. A
third says the *Rowley-Powley* burden must be much older than Liston,

melody will recognize at once that the tune of this version has
not the true hallmark, but rather the music hall mark, upon it.
I also found a sheet music form of this version in the Library

---

since he had seen the old words *rowley powley* defined somewhere as a
plump fowl, "of which," he facetiously remarks, "gammon and spinach
are posthumous connexions." *(Cf. roly poly* in New English Dictionary.)
The fourth correspondent gives on p. 75 of this same issue the Irish
version (reprinted above), remarking that the air (which he unfortunately does not give) was exceedingly quaint and seemed to have the
stamp of antiquity. In the July 13, 1850, issue (II, 110), still another
correspondent says that the Irish version recently reported was only a
modern variant of a ballad which he remembered to have heard sixty
years before (this would be about 1790, or two decades before Liston's
song) and which began,

> There was a frog lived in a well,
>> *Heigho crowdie!*
> And a merry mouse in a mill
>> *With a howdie crowdie, &c. &c.*

> The frog he would a-wooing go,
>> *Heigho crowdie!*
> Whether his mother would let him or no,
>> *With a howdie crowdie, &c. &c.*

Kittredge queries whether this is the original of the Liston burden.
On August 17, 1850 (II, 188), comes still another who states that when
he was a boy he heard an old aunt repeatedly sing the song with a
strange chorus; he gives the earliest reference to the *Kimo* (or *Kymy)*
burden that I have found.

> A frog he would a-wooing ride,
>> *With a rigtum bullydimy kymy;*
> With sword and buckler by his side,
>> *With a rigdum bullydimy kymy.*

> *Kymyary kalty cary*
> *Kymyary kymy*
> *Strimstram paradiddly larrabona ringting,*
>> *Rigdum bullydimy kymy.*

Finally in the January 25, 1851, issue (III, 51), Edward F. Rimbault
points out that the original of the popular song referred to in the several
previous issues was to be found in Ravenscroft's *Melismata* (1611),
giving the song as printed there. After this central shot from the scholar
the chatter of the correspondents in *Notes and Queries* suddenly ceased.
It should be added, however, that there are several additional references
to the origin and application of the words *Rowley* and *Powley* in the First
Series of *Notes and Queries*. See I, 250, 457; III, 28; IX, 235, 477;
X, 274, for reference to *Rowley;* and for notes on *Powley*, see I, 214, 282,
370; II, 76.

of Congress. It was published some time about 1860 by Parker and Ditson, Boston, and described as "a sentimental song, written and composed by one John Smith." I take it that the ascription of the authorship to "one John Smith" was the publishers' surreptitious way of advertising the song as a new production, or perhaps as a folk-song, the folk being represented by the ubiquitous "John Smith." While the music of this version has had but little influence on the popular American versions,[4] I reproduce it (from a photostat of the sheet music version in the Library of Congress) for purposes of comparison.

---

[4]But see Texas version No. 11 below.

BOSTON: Published by PARKER & DITSON 135 Washington Street.   *18 -*

Whether his mother would let him or no, With a Row__ly Pow__ly Gammon and Spinage O heigh said An_tho_ny Rowly.

2
Off he set with his Opera Hat,
 Heigh ho &c.
On the road he met with a Rat,
 With a Rowly Powly &c.

3
They soon arriv'd at the Mouses Hall,
 Heigh ho &c.
They gave a loud tap and they gave a loud call,
 With a Rowly Powly &c

Pray Mrs. Mouse are you within,
 Heigh ho &c.
Yes kind sirs, I'm sitting to spin,
 With a Rowly Powly &c.

Come Mrs. Mouse now give us some beer,
 Heigh ho &c,
That Froggy and I may have some cheer,
 With a Rowly Powly &c.

6
Pray Mr. Frog will you give us a song,
 Heigh ho &c.
Let the subject be something that's not very long,
 With a Rowly Powly &c.

7
Indeed Mrs. Mouse replied the Frog,
 Heigh ho &c.
A cold has made me as hoarse as a hog,
 With a Rowly Powly &c.

Since you have caught cold Mr. Frog, Mousy said,
 Heigh ho &c.
I'll sing you a song that I have just made,
 With a Rowly Powly &c,

9
As they were in glee and a merry making,
 Heigh ho &c.
A Cat and her Kittens came tumbling in,
 With a Rowly Powly &c,

10
The Cat she seized the Rat by the Crown,
 Heigh ho &c.
The Kittens they pulled the little Mouse down,
 With a Rowly Powly &c.

11
This put Mr. Frog in a terrible fright,
 Heigh ho &c.
He took up his hat and he wished them good night,
 With a Rowly Powly &c.

12
As Froggy was crossing it over a brook,
 Heigh ho &c.
A lilly white Duck came and gobbled him up,
 With a Rowly Powly &c.

13
So here is an end to one, two, three,
 Heigh ho &c.
The Rat, the Mouse, and little Froggy,
 With a Rowly Powly &c,

III. THE TEXAS VERSIONS

A few years ago I accidentally came upon two or three
Mother Goose rhymes which were frequently used in Texas as
nursery songs to amuse children or soothe them into slumber.
In 1923 I reported these to the Texas Folk-Lore Society in a
paper entitled "Some Texas Popular Songs."   Upon the suggestion of Dr. Louise Pound, who had heard the paper, I made
some further investigations into the origin and the local distribution of one of these, "The Frog's Courting," and of this
song collected some thirty-odd versions, mainly from my students in the University of Texas.   I was surprised to find
that approximately half of my students had heard the song
(60 per cent in one class) though only a few of them remembered it well enough to write out the versions they had heard.
I also made some investigations into the history of the song,
but I had not gone far in my quest when the belated October-
December, 1922, number of the *Journal of American Folk-Lore*
appeared with the extensive "Traditional Texts and Tunes"
article by Professor A. H. Tolman and Miss Mary O. Eddy.
In this article I found two additional versions, similar to
several of my own, reported by Miss Eddy from Ohio, and
a full note by Professor Kittredge on the history of this well-
known song.   I confess that before I had read Professor Kittredge's note I had no idea of the wide distribution and the
many divagations and ramifications of the song.   The references which he gives fill five and a half large pages in the
Tolman-Eddy article (pp. 394-399, JAFL, Vol. XXXV, No.
138).   Though I worked up the principal references inde-
pendently, my notes on the history of the song summarized
above are almost all included in Professor Kittredge's surpris-
ing array of facts concerning the song in its various forms.

It has been difficult to find a satisfactory basis of classification for the Texas versions, but I have hit upon the device
of grouping them according to the variations in the burden,
for a change in the burden usually indicates a change in the
tune.   Apparently, the older versions have more elaborate
nonsense burdens, and the later American versions avoid the
difficulty of the more complex nonsense syllables by substi-
tuting a mere humming burden in the unspellable *uhn-huhn*

(or with lips closed *uhm-huhm)* syllables. This last type, doubtless because it is more easily remembered and because it affords an excellent humming tune for lullaby purposes, is by far the most popular of the Texas versions. However, the fact that the *uhn-huhn* burden is found only in the South or in versions originating in the South suggests another explanation—namely, that the negro mammies, who frequently sang the song in the old South, were unequal to the repetition of the nonsense jingle and substituted the *uhn-huhn* humming chorus, which, as is well known, is a notable characteristic of negro music.

I have made six types on the burden basis: The A type, or *tiddle-lum* burden, having one version; the B type, or the *Kitty-alone* burden, showing four versions; the C type, or the *kimo-karo* burden, showing eight versions; the D type, or the *O-gang* burden, with one version; the E type, or the *uhn-huhn* burden, showing twenty-odd versions; and finally a negro version, which I have called the F type, with the *ta-da-tee-dee* burden.

A. (1) The Texas version that is perhaps nearest the *Melismata* tune shows similarity to the *tweedle-tweedle* burden[5] in the *tiddle lum tiddle larry* variation; it was supplied by Miss Fannie M. Bouton, Webster, Texas.[6] She took the song down from her grandmother, Mrs. Margaret I. Wifer (born in Greenville, Illinois, 1838), who learned it from her mother, Mrs. Mary White (*née* Denny in 1794), a native of North Carolina. The tune and words follow:

1   There was a frog in yonder well,
     Fa lee linkum larry,[7]

---

[5]See also the *tweedle-tweedle* burden of No. 6 below.

[6]There is also some similarity in the words of this version and those of the Irish version on p. 9 above.

[7]The burden of this version is quite similar to that of Mrs. Leather's Irish nurse version in *Folk-Lore of Herefordshire* (1912), p. 210.

And a mouse in yonder mill,
  Tiddle lum tiddle larry.

2 The frog he rose and he must ride,
   With sword and buckler by his side.

3 He rode till he came to the miller's door;
   There he did both knock and roar.

4 "Miss Mouse, are you within?"
   "Yes, kind sir, I sit and spin."

5 "Is your Uncle Rat at home?"
   "No, he's gone to see his son."

6 Old Uncle Rat came rattling home,
   "Who's been here since I've been gone?"

7 " 'Twas a handsome, tall young man,
   Swears he'll have me if he can."

8 "Change a farthing, bring the wine,
   That we may all eat and drink and dine."

9 In came a mole so black,
   With the fiddle on his back.

10 In came the bumblebee,
    Took the fiddle on his knee.

11 In came the hopping flea,
    He could dance courageously.

12 In came the clawed cat,
    Took Miss Mousie by the back.

13 Old Uncle Rat ran up the wall,
    "I believe the devil's among you all."

14 The frog he leaped toward the brook,
    There he met with a hungry duck.

15 The duck she swallowed him down her crook,
    And that's the end of my history book.

  B. (2) In the B type, with the *Kitty-alone* burden, I have
four versions. The first of these is from H. W. Hinkle, Genoa,
Texas, who comes from Illinois, if I remember correctly. This

version, like No. 1 above, is notable for repeating the line of
the 1549 reference ("The Frog Cam to the myl dur") nearly in
the original form—"He rode up to the mill house door." The
Kitty-alone burden suggests kinship with the Scotch *Cuddy-
alone* burden in the Harvard MS. versions reported by Professor Kittredge; and the introduction of *Colleen MacCarey*
(for the *Cock me cary* of the Ritson-Halliwell burden) suggests Irish antecedents. This is the only version I have seen
which calls the frog a toad(y) and gives so full a description
of him. I heard Mr. Hinkle sing the eight stanzas of this
version in a tune suggestive of the plaintive notes of the
bagpipe, but I have been unable as yet to secure the exact score
of his tune.

1 Toady took a thought to ride,
  Kitty alone, Kitty alone,
  Kitty alone and I.
  Toady took a thought to ride,
  Sword and pistol by his side,
    Colleen MacCarey, Kitty alone,
    Kitty alone and I.

2 He rode up to the mill house door,
  And very loudly he did roar.

3 "Lady Mouse, are you within?"
  "Yes, and I can card and spin."

4 He said, "Lady Mouse, will you marry me?"
  "Yes, if Uncle Rat will agree."

5 Uncle Rat came rattling home,
  "Who's been here since I've been gone?"

6 "I've had a suitor for my hand;
  He says he'll marry me if he can."

7 "What kind of looking man was he?"
  Uncle Rat he said, said he.

8 "Long legs and forked toes,
  Broken back and speckled clothes."

(3) My second *Kitty-alone* version in two forms, *(a)* and
(b), is particularly full (sixteen stanzas) and has a very attractive tune. The first form of this version (3a) I got

from Mrs. Harriet Harper Cox, now of Galveston, but formerly of Williamson County, near Austin; and later I secured a slightly variant version (3*b*) from her aunts, Mrs. Olivia LeSueur Moore, of Austin, and Mrs. Addie LeSueur Mahan, now of Chicago. This latter version comes from Mrs. Cox's grandmother, Mrs. Annie LeSueur (*née* Nowlin), who was an old-fashioned, but quite cultivated, singing mother of Williamson and Travis counties. I give only one form, (3*b*). The *Rock and Kay* of this burden is evidently a softened form of the *Cock me cary* (perhaps through the intermediate form "Rock and Rye") of the Ritson-Halliwell version. Mrs. Moore, who gave me the melody, says she thinks the song has been in her family on her mother's side for five or six generations. The music is very soothing, having, it seems to me, like Mr. Hinkle's version, a distinct reminiscence of the bagpipe drone, particularly in the minor strains.

1 Frog went a-courting, he did ride,
   Kitty alone, Kitty alone;
Frog went a-courting, he did ride,
   Kitty alone and I;
Frog went a-courting, he did ride,
Sword and pistol by his side,
   Rock and Kay, Kitty alone,
   Kitty alone and I.

2 Frog went down to Miss Mouse's hall,
And there he stood and loudly called.

3 Says he, "Miss Mouse, are you within?"
   "Yes, kind sir, I sit and spin."

4 Frog fell down upon his knee,
   "Oh, Miss Mouse, will you marry me?"

5 "Not without Uncle Rat's consent,
   Would I marry the President."

6 Uncle Rat he laughed and smiled,
   To think his niece would be a bride.

7 Uncle Rat he went to town
   To buy his niece a wedding gown.

8 Where shall the wedding supper be?
   Way down yonder in a hollow tree.

9 What shall the wedding supper be?
   A black-eyed pea and a bumblebee.

10 The first that came was Colonel Tick,
    Walking with his hickory stick.

11 The next that came was Major Bee,
    With his fiddle on his knee.

12 The next that came was a broken-back flea
    To dance the jig with Major Bee.

13 Then came the man up from the brook,[8]
    To marry them out of his little book.

14 Frog went sailing 'cross the lake,
    And he was bit up by a big black snake.

15 The big black snake he swam to land,
    And he was killed by a big French man.

16 The big French man he went to France,
    And that's the end of this romance.[9]

(4) A third version with the *Kitty-alone* burden comes
from Professor John W. Calhoun, of Austin. He calls this

---

[8]Another version (No. 28) gives *minnow* for *man up*, an interesting
example of folk etymology or mistaken word identity.

[9]Mrs. Cox's version (3*a*) shows but slight variations. See note on **MS.**
additions at end of this article.

"a Middle Tennessee version, Southern Hills." He learned it
in his family in East Texas some forty years ago. The tune
is a familiar play-party melody adapted to the frog-mouse
words. Mr. Calhoun says his family also sang the same words
to the more familiar tune (see E type below) with the *uhn-huhn* burden.

1   A frog went a-courtin' and he did ride,
   Kitty alone, Kitty alone,
A sword and a pistol by his side,
   Kitty alone and I.

2   He rode till he came to the Mouse's door,
And there he jumped upon the floor.

3   He took little Mousie on his knee,
And said, "Little Mouse, will you marry me?"

4   "Oh, no, Frog, I can't do that
Without consent of Uncle Rat."

5   Old Uncle Rat came galloping home,
Saying, "Who's been here since I've been gone?"

(Some lines are missing here.)

6   Where shall the wedding supper be?
Way down yonder in a hollow beech tree.

7   What shall the wedding supper be
The two hind-quarters of a bumblebee.

8   The first came in was Squire Snail,
With the license on his tail.

9   The next came in was a little snake,
With his tea and his cake.

10 The next came in was the bumblebee,
With a banjo on his knee.

11 The next came in was the hoppin' flea,
    To dance a jig with the bumblebee.

12 The next came in was an old tomcat,
    And he put an end to all of that.

13 Old Uncle Rat he scaled the wall,
    His foot slipped and he caught a fall.

14 The frog went swimmin' down the lake,
    And there he met with a hungry snake.

15 The black snake swallowed him down his crook,
    And that is the end of the little song book.

The fourth version is a mere fragment which was handed to me by Mrs. A. O. Stevens, the wife of a Unitarian minister of Austin. She said she learned the song in Missouri in her childhood days. The single stanza she gave me is set in an attractive minor key, tune similar to that of No. 3 above.

Rock me cary, Kity alone, Kitty alone, Kitty alone,
Rock me cary, Kitty alone, Kitty alone and I.
    Uncle Rat came riding down
    In his silk and satin gown,
Rock me cary, Kitty alone, Kitty alone and I.

C. (5) The C type has the more elaborate *Kimo-karo* burden. I have eight versions of this type, though two of them are mere fragments. The first fragment comes directly from Maine through the wife of a professor in the University

of Texas, Mrs. W. T. Mather, formerly of the district near
Bangor, who learned the song about 1870 from her mother,
Mrs. Helen Marquis Nevine.   The tune and words were handed
down through a grandmother, Elizabeth Linnell, a native of
Maine, and a great-grandmother, Mary Campbell, from Scot-
land.   This version is distinctive as one of the few American
versions using "a-wooing go" for the usual "a-courting ride."
Mrs. Mather recalls the first stanza perfectly, but can recall
only snatches of the remaining stanzas, such as "Mistress
Mouse, are you within?" and "Yes, kind sir, I sit to spin."
Her first stanza with tune is as follows:

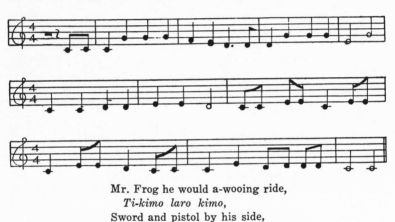

Mr. Frog he would a-wooing ride,
   Ti-kimo laro kimo,
Sword and pistol by his side,
   Bottominy winktumy,
   Rinktum-y-ray,
   Tummi rinktum,
   Bottominy kimo.

(6)   The second fragmentary version is notable in that
it repeats the *tweedle-tweedle* burden of the *Melismata* tune,
though it is plainly closely related to the later American versions in both words and tune.   I obtained this fragment from
Mr. Carl Kemp, a student at the time in the West Texas State
Teachers' College, Canyon, Texas; he says he learned the tune
from relatives who came from Arkansas into Central and West
Texas.   It is as follows:

A frog went a-courting, and he did ride,
With a tweedle, tweedle, tweedle,
He got swallowed by a big black snake,
With a humpty dumpty deedle.

Kimo Karo, Captain Karo,
Kimo Karo kimo,
Lattibota rinktum,
Runsacka bolten kimo.[10]

(7)   The third example of this type was given to me by
Mr. R. A. Cox, Instructor in Economics, University of Texas,
who learned it from his mother, Mrs. R. Y. Cox, of Tipper
County (near Corinth), Mississippi. She learned it, in her
childhood before the Civil War, from her mother, who was

---

[10]Miss Morelza Morrow, the student who put me on the track of this
version, says that she heard her little brother, who learned the song
from Carl Kemp, sing it as follows:

A frog went a-courting, he did ride,
Tweedle tweedle tweedle;
He got swallowed by a big black snake,
And a humpty dumpty deedle.
Captain Karo, kimonaro,
Captain Karo kimo,
Rotobota rinktum,
Ransacka botum kimo.

This shows the variations likely to occur even in the first removal.

formerly Mary Green, of St. Clair County, Alabama. The
tune of this version is practically the same as that of Mr.
Lowe's version (next to be given) but without the elaborate
kimonaro chorus following the stanza.

1 Mr. Frog went a-courting, he did ride,
    Latter butter rinktum kimeo,
  Sword and pistol by his side,
    Latter butter rinktum rinktum rinktum kimeo.

2 He rode up to Miss Mouse's house,
  "Say, Miss Mouse, will you marry me?"

3 Mr. Rat did laugh and shake his fat sides
  To think his niece would be a bride.

4 Where shall the wedding supper be?
  Way over yonder in a hollow tree.

5 What shall the wedding supper be?
  Black-eyed peas and bread and butter.

6 First one in was Mr. Bee,
  Danced a jig with a bumble bee.

7 Next one in was Captain Snake,
  Ate up all the wedding cake.

(8)   The fourth example of this type is from Mr. Louis
Lowe, of Taylor, Williamson County, Texas. He says he has
sung the song as long as he can remember, and he is now in
his fifties. He was born and reared in West Texas near San
Angelo, but his parents came from Alabama and Mississippi.
His version is as follows:

1 Frog went a-courtin', he did ride,
    Rigtum butty middy kimo,

Sword and a pistol by his side,
Rigtum butty middy kimo.

Kimynaro karo gilto,
Ki-mortem strimmy strummy,
Bubbadillo lallibubby;
Digtum rigtum butty middy kimo.[11]

2 What shall the wedding supper be?
Two butter-beans and a black-eyed pea.

3 First come in was a flying moth,
For to spread the tablecloth.

4 Next come in was a rattlesnake
With the coffee and the cake.

5 Next come in was a bumblebee
With his fiddle on his knee.[12]

(9) Dr. Killis Campbell, of the University of Texas, secured the following version (fifth of this type) from his sister-in-law, Mrs. Hawes Campbell, Enfield, King William County, Virginia.[13] She says this is the version which "Mother" Campbell sang in Virginia many years ago. I have not as yet secured the tune to her version, but I imagine it is similar to the tunes of the other versions in this section. Her version adds a feature not found in any other version I have seen, namely, the bride's and groom's costumes (stanzas 11 and 12).

1 Froggie went a-courtin', and he did ride,
Rigtum mollie kitcha krimeo,
Sword and pistol by his side,
Rigtum mollie kitcha krimeo.

---

[11]Mr. Newton Gaines reports a senior class high-school yell from Fort Worth (1907–08) which is doubtless based on the several forms of this burden:

Keemo kimo-karro warro
Timeo timeo
Rum skum fumadiddle
Singsong kitty
Won't you kimeo
Seniors, Seniors, wow sis boom, kuku.

[12]This fragmentary version was the first which I found, the one which started me in my quest of Mr. Frog and Miss Mouse.

[13]Another version from this family (No. 36) with the *uhn-huhn* burden was transcribed for me by Mrs. Hawes Campbell's daughter, Ellie.

Krimeo, krimeo,
Hi manaro deltum karo,
Rigtum mollie kitcha marabo,
Rigtum rigtum mollie kitcha krimeo.

2   He rode up to Miss Mouse's hall,
And there he paid a regular call.

3   Lord Rat met him at the door
And proudly escorted him across the floor.

4   He took Miss Mousie upon his knee,
"O pray, Miss Mousie, will you marry me?"

5   "O yes, if Uncle Rat will agree,
Agree for you to marry me."

6   Uncle Rat he rode to town,
To buy his niece a wedding gown.

7   Pray, where is the wedding going to be?
Away down yonder in a hollow tree.

8   The first to come was Captain Juney Bug;
He took his seat by the whiskey jug.

9   The next to come was Mrs. Cow;
She made a very graceful bow.

10   The next to come was Mrs. Flea;
She danced a jig with the bumblebee.

11   Pray, what was the bride dressed in?
A cream gauze veil and a brass breastpin.

12   Pray, what was the groom dressed in?
Sky blue britches with silver stitches.

13   What did they have for the wedding supper?
Black-eyed peas and bread and butter.

14   They all sat down and began to chat,
When in walked the kitten and the cat.

15   The cat grabbed Lord Rat by the crown,
While the kitten tossed Miss Mousie up and down.

16   The frog he swam across the lake,
Was swallowed by a long black snake.

17　This is the last of one, two, three,
　　The rat, the frog, and the little mousie.

(10)　The sixth example of the C type is in two versions *(a)* and *(b)*, one supplied by Dr. B. C. Tharp, Associate Professor of Botany in the University of Texas, and another by his sister, Mrs. John M. Neal, of Huntsville, Texas.　Dr. Tharp says that he and his sisters learned the song about 1890 from their parents, both of whom are native Georgians, and from the Stevenses, a family who lived in the neighborhood and were much given to ballad singing.　Dr. Tharp's mother says she learned the piece sixty years ago in Georgia, but that she does not remember from whom she learned it.　Mrs. Neal's version is fuller, and, as Dr. Tharp says, much more accurate, and hence I give it first.

1　A frog went a-courtin', he did ride,
　　Ringtum bottle and a kymo,
　Sword and pistol by his side,
　　Ringtum bottle and a kymo.

　　O my nero, giltuma garo,
　　O my nero garo,
　　Shem shem sham, and a shatter patter rangtang,
　　Ringtum bottle and a kymo.[14]

---

[14]The burden of the Tharp versions is related to the burden of Mrs. Leather's first fragmentary version, *Folk-lore of Herefordshire* (1912), p. 209.

2   He rode up to Miss Mouse's hall,
    Loud and lovely did he call.

3   Said he, "Miss Mousie, may I come in?"
    "Yes, come in and see me spin."

4   He took Miss Mousie upon his knee,
    Said he, "Miss Mousie, will you marry me?"

5   "Not without Uncle Rat's consent,
    Do you think I'd marry the President?"

6   Uncle Rat gave his consent,
    Cousin Cat her parlor lent.

7   Where shall the weddin' supper be?
    Way down yonder in the old hollow tree.

8   What shall the weddin' supper be?
    Three green beans and a black-eyed pea.

9   The first to come in was a big black snake,
    A-wantin' a piece of the weddin' cake.

10 The next to come in was the bumblebee,
    With his fiddle on his knee.

11 The next to come in was a big black bug,
    With his rum in his jug.

12 The last to come in was a skippin' flea,
    To dance a jig with the bumblebee.

13 While they were all a-eatin' supper,
    The cat came in and made 'em all scatter.

14 Old Uncle Rat ran up the wall,
    Thinkin' Old Scratch was among them all.

15 Little Miss Mouse ran under the bed;
    Once in a while she'd poke out her head.

16 The frog he jumped into the lake;
    He was swallowed by a big black snake.

17 The big black snake he swam to land,
    And he was killed by a big black man.

18 The big black man has gone to France,
    So this is the end of our romance.

(10b) Dr. Tharp's version follows:

1 A frog went a-courtin', he did ride,
      Ringtum bottle and a kymo,
   Sword and pistol by his side,
      Ringtum bottle and a kymo.

      O my daro, giltuma garo,
      O my daro garo,
      Shim shim sham and a shatter patter rangtang,
      Ringtum bottle and a kymo.

2 He rode up to Miss Mousie's side,
   Said he, "Miss Mousie, will you be my bride?"
      (*Or*, He rode up to Miss Mousie's den,
      Said he, "Miss Mousie, are you in?")

3 He took Miss Mousie on his knee,
   Said he, "Miss Mousie, will you marry me?"

4 "Not without Uncle Rat's consent
   Would I marry the President."

5 Uncle Rat gave his consent,
   Cousin Cat her parlor lent.

6 Where shall the weddin' supper be?
   Way down yonder in the old hollow tree.

7 What shall the weddin' supper be?
   A big fat fly and a black-eyed pea.

8 The first fine guest was a big black bug,
   With his rum in his jug.

9 The next fine guest was a bumblebee,
   With his fiddle on his knee.

10 While they were all a-eatin' supper,
    The cat came and made 'em all scatter.

11 The frog he jumped into a lake,
    And there was swallowed by a big black snake.

12 The mousie hid upon a shelf,
    And if you want any more, you may sing it yourself.

(11)   The seventh example of the C type is a fragment coming from New York *via* Connecticut.   Professor Thad Riker, of the History Department of the University of Texas, heard a maiden aunt sing this version in his childhood and recalls a few stanzas with the tune.   It is a curious mixture of the traditional and the Liston stage versions.

1   A frog he would a-wooing go,
   Singsong polly mitchy kimo,[15]
  Whether his mother would let him or no,
   Singsong polly mitchy kimo.

   Kimo karo danso wherro,
   Kimo kimo karo,
   Pummy little, pummy little, pummy little,
    pummy little,
   Linkum polly mitchy kimo.[15]

---

[15]*Linkum matty mitty kimo* was sometimes substituted, says Mr. Riker. This chorus is doubtless related to Christy and Wood's "a celebrated banjo song" called "Keemo Kimo" with interlined refrain "Sing Song Kitty, can't you Ki Me O!" and with the following chorus:
     Keemo Kimo, dar, Oh whar!
     Wid my hi, my ho, and in come Sally singing
     Sometimes penny winkle, linktum nipcat
     Sing Song Kitty, can't you Ki Me O!
Found in Christy and Wood's *New Song Book*, 1854.   Quoted in Dorothy Scarborough's *On the Trail of Negro Folk-Songs*, Cambridge, 1925, p. 285.   On page 156 of her book Miss Scarborough gives another lullaby which has a tune and words quite similar to those in Mr. Riker's chorus, particularly "Pompey doodle sing song Polly witch o-crimeo" and "Singsong-Polly, won't you ki' me oh."

2 Then froggie put on his best new hat,
   And on the way he met a rat.

3 And when they came to the mouse's hall
   Then they did so loudly call.

4 "Oh, Mrs. Mouse, are you within?"
   "Oh, yes, kind sir, I am learning to spin."

(12)   This eighth version of the C type comes from Miss Thisbe Worley, of San Antonio, through her mother. The family came from Kentucky to Texas about 1876. The last three stanzas were sung in a variety of forms, says Miss Worley, to suit the whims of the children.

1 Frog went a-courtin', he did ride,
   Laddie bunny rigdom kimo.
   Frog went a-courtin', he did ride,
   A sword and pistol by his side,
   Laddie bunny rigdom kimo.

      Kimo, nero, Captain Kero,
      Kimo, nero, kimo,
      Samma natcha, bomma natcha,
      Laddie bunny rigdom, rigdom, rigdom,
      Laddie bunny rigdom kimo.

2 He rode up to Miss Mousie's hall,
   And there he did both knock and call.

3 Sez he, "Is Lady Mouse within?"
   "Yes, indeed, I sit and spin."

4 He took Lady Mouse upon his knee,
   Sez he, "Lady Mouse, will you marry me?"

5 "Not without Uncle Rat's consent
   Would I marry the President."

6 Uncle Rat laughed and shook his fat sides
   To think his niece would soon be a bride.

7 Oh, where shall the wedding supper be?
   Way down yonder in a hollow tree.

8 And what shall the wedding supper be?
   Two butter-beans and a black-eyed pea.

9   First came in was a big black snake
    With a pound and a half of wedding cake.

10 Then came in a nimble flea
    To dance a jig with a bumblebee.

11 Next came in was a big black bug,
    Passin' all around with a whiskey jug.

12 Lady Mouse went skippin' through the field,
    She fell down and skinned her heel.

13 Uncle Rat tried to cross the lake,
    He got swallowed by the big black snake.

14 Froggie croaked himself away,
    And that was the end of his wedding day.

D.   (13)   The single short version in my D group shows an entirely new burden, which I have called the *O-gang* type. This version comes from a fifth-grade pupil (Vera Mae Slaughter) in the Farrar School, Limestone County, Texas. I have been unable to secure the tune or trace the source of this version, but I judge that it is merely a variation of the very common *uhn-huhn* burden of the E type below. It goes as follows:

1   Frog went a-courting, and he did ride,
        O gang;
    Frog went a-courting, and he did ride,
    Sword and pistol by his side,
        O gang gang gilly wally ging time,
        Goo-i goo-i goo gang goo.

2   He rode up to Miss Mouse's door,
    Rapped so hard till he made it roar.

3   He took Miss Mousie on his knee,
    Said, "My girl, will you marry me?"

4   "Oh, I can't tell you about that;
    You'll have to see old Daddy Rat."

5   Old Daddy Rat has gone to town,
    To buy his daughter a wedding gown.

6   Where shall the wedding supper be?
    Way down yonder in a hollow tree.

7 What shall the wedding supper be?
Roasted cob and cup of tea.

E. (14) By far the most numerous group is the E type
with the *uhn-huhn,* or humming, burden. I have collected
twenty-odd versions of this type, the only value of so large a
number being to show that there are probably no two versions
of the song exactly alike, even when sung by members of the
same family. The common form of this tune may be illustrated by Mr. Newton Gaines's (of Fort Worth, Texas) version. He says: "The following was taught me by my aunt,
Miss Porcher Gaines, who learned it from her mother, who
probably learned it in either eastern Tennessee or Georgia before the Civil War." It opens with "Froggie would a-wooing
go" of the Liston stage song, but immediately following is the
common American opening, "Froggie went a-courting."

1 Froggie would a-wooing go,
  Uhn-huhn;
  Froggie would a-wooing go,
  Whether his mother said yes or no,
  Uhn-huhn.

2 Froggie went courting, and he did ride,
  A sword and a pistol by his side.

3 He stopped at Mistress Mousie's door,
  And aloud he did roar.

4 "Oh, say, Miss Mouse, are you within?"
  Yes, Miss Mouse did sit and spin.

5 He took Miss Mouse upon his knee,
  And he said, "Miss Mouse, will you marry me?"

6 "Not without Uncle Rat's consent,
  I wouldn't marry the President."

7 Old Uncle Rat he laughed till he cried,
  To think his niece would be a bride.

8   Where shall the wedding supper be?
    Way down yonder in the hollow tree.

9   What shall the wedding supper be?
    Two teacakes and a cup of tea.

10 First came in was a bumblebee,
    And he tuned his fiddle on his knee.

11 Next came in was Captain Tick,
    And he ate so much that it made him sick.

12 Next came in was an old black snake,
    To pass around the wedding cake.

13 Next came in was Doctor Fly,
    And he said, "Young fellow, I think you'll die."

14 Next came in was an old gray cat,
    And soon she put a stop to that.

15 She grabbed 'em up, one, two, three,
    The frog and the mouse and the bumblebee.[16]

(15)   Occasionally a slightly different tune is given, as in
the version from Mr. John C. Bridgewater, of Chocolate Bayou,
Texas, now an old man.   He learned the song when he was a
small boy in Tennessee, and he says that his sister informs
him that the family learned the words and tune from a travel-
ing singer.   His version of eighteen stanzas goes like this:

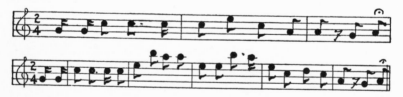

------

[16]Mr. Gaines has improvised dramatic gestures and imitations similar
to those in the Battle version (No. 19) below.
    Miss Dorothy Scarborough in her *On the Trail of Negro Folk Songs*
(1925) gives three versions of 13, 5, and 13 stanzas, respectively,
all with the *uhn-huhn* burden (pp. 46-50).   Mr. John Harrington Cox
in his *Folk-Songs of the South* (1924) prints three versions, with three
burdens, *Tappin,'* *M-m-m-huh,* and *Tid-e-ra-e-ral, tid-e-ra-e-ral, ding-
dong-de-day* respectively.   He notes four other versions and gives *To
diddle de dum, To diddle de dum* as burden for one of these (pp. 470-473).

1 Mr. Frog went a-courting, and he did ride,
   Eh-heh.[17]
  Mr. Frog went a-courting, and he did ride,
  With a sword and pistol at his side,
   Eh-heh.

2 He rode up to Miss Mouse's door
  Where often he had been before.

3 He rode up to Miss Mouse's hall,
  And loudly tapped and loud did call.

4 "Oh, who's within; oh, who's within?"
  "Alight, Mr. Frog, and do come in."

5 He took Miss Mousie upon his knee,
  And said, "Miss Mouse, will you marry me?"

6 "No, kind sir, I can't tell that
  Without consent of Uncle Rat."

7 Uncle Rat at last when he came home,
  Said, "Who's been here since I've been gone?"

8 "A very fine gentleman has been here,
  Who wishes me to be his dear."

9 Uncle Rat laughed and shook his fat side
  To think his niece would be a bride.

10 Straightway he hopped away to town
  To buy his niece a wedding gown.

11 Oh, where shall the wedding supper be?
  Away down yonder in a hollow tree.

12 What shall we have for the wedding supper?
  Two big peas 'thout a bit of butter.

13 The first one there was Pussy Cat,
  To lead the dance with Uncle Rat.

14 Miss Mouse went a-skipping up the wall,
  Her foot made a slip, and she got a fall.

15 The next one came was Colonel Flea,
  Who had his banjo on his knee.

---

[17]The *uhn-huhn* syllables are sometimes doubled, and in some versions changed to *eh-heh*, as here.

16   The next one there was Bumblebee,
     To dance a jig with Colonel Flea.

17   They all went sailing across the lake
     And three got swallowed by a big black snake.

18   This is the end of one, two, three,
     The frog, the mouse, and the bumblebee.

(16)   Mrs. E. C. Gordon, now an old woman, of Columbus, Texas, supplies the following version. She is a native of northern Mississippi and learned the song in her childhood in that state. Her mother came from South Carolina and her father from North Carolina. She does not know from which branch of the family the song originally came, but she says it has been sung to the children for at least five generations. She asserts that her grandmother sang the song to her mother ninety years ago; she herself put her little ones to sleep with it sixty years ago, and she is now singing it to her grandchildren in the same way. The tune to her version is in slow time, and the song, when sung by a mother's soothing voice, doubtless afforded a fine charm to Morpheus.

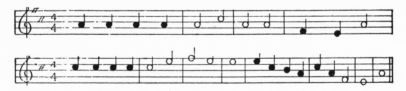

1   Mr. Frog went a-courting, he did ride,
       Uh-huhn,
    Mr. Frog went a-courting, he did ride,
    A sword and a pistol by his side,
       Uh-huhn.

2   He rode up to Miss Mousie's door,
    Where he'd often been before.

3   He said, "Miss Mousie, may I come in,
    And sit right where you card and spin?"

4   He took Miss Mousie upon his knee,
    And said, "Miss Mousie, will you marry me?"

5   "Not without Uncle's Rat's consent
    Would I marry the President."

6   Neat Uncle Rat came a-bustling in [on?],
     "And who's been here since I've been gone?"

7   "A pretty young man, and he came in
     And sat right where I card and spin."

8   Uncle Rat laughed and shook his fat sides
     To think his niece would soon be a bride.

9   Neat Uncle Rat he went to town
     To buy his niece a wedding gown.

10   Where shall the wedding supper be?
     Away down yonder in a hollow tree.

11   What shall the wedding supper be?
     Three green beans and a black-eyed pea.

12   The first came in was a bumblebee,
     To play the fiddle upon his knee.

13   Next came in was a Mr. Flea,
     To dance a jig with the bumblebee.

14   Miss Cat she stepped in to supper,
     And turned over the plate of butter.

15   Miss Mousie went a-tearing up the wall,
     Her foot 'slipped and she got a fall.

16   Mr. Frog went a-sailing 'cross the lake,
     And he was swallowed by a big black snake.

17   So here's the end of one, two, three,
     The cat, the frog, and Miss Mousie.

18   The knife and the fork are on the shelf,
     You want any more, just sing it yourself.

(17)   A peculiar variation of the *uhn-huhn* burden is the attempt to imitate the gurgling sound of a bullfrog. The following version was given to me by one of my students, Miss Gladys Peeler, of Dallas. She learned it from her mother, who, she thinks, picked up the peculiar variation of the burden from friends around Dallas. The sound is made low down in the throat by a strange subglottal contraction of the vocal chords. It is impossible to describe or spell out the syllables, but I

have made an attempt to suggest the sound by the form *ach-ghuuooh.*[18]

1   A frog went a-courting, and he did ride,
      Ach-ghuuooh;
    A frog went a-courting, and he did ride,
    With a sword and pistol by his side,
      Ach-ghuuooh, ach-ghuuooh, ach-ghuuooh,
      ach-ghuuooh.

2   He rode up to Miss Mouse's hall,
    And there he did so loudly call.

3   He took Miss Mousie on his knee,
    And said to her, "Will you marry me?"

4   Old Uncle Rat he shook his fat side,
    To think his niece would be a bride.

5   Old Uncle Rat he went to town,
    To buy his niece a wedding gown.

6   Where shall the wedding supper be?
    Away down yonder in a hollow tree.

7   What shall the wedding supper be?
    Three green beans and a black-eyed pea.

8   The first one to come was a bumblebee,
    With his fiddle on his knee.

9   The next one to come was a big black bug,
    With his little whiskey jug.

10 The next one to come was a minnow from the brook,
    To marry Miss Mousie with his book.

(18)   A similar imitation of the sound of the frog's croak is found in a version contributed by Miss Kathryn Webb, of Waco, whose grandparents brought the song into Texas from

---

[18]My MS. versions 39 *a* and *b* and 40 seem to have a similar imitation of the sound made by a frog. No. 39, supplied in two forms, *(b)* by Miss Edna McCormick, of San Marcos, and *(a)* by her mother, Mrs. W. L. McCormick, of Denton, shows two burdens, *And a humpgh* and *And a kum,* which are described as being sung deep in the throat, apparently in imitation of the croak of a frog. No. 40, from Mrs. R. T. Pritchett, of Corpus Christi, had *Ump! Humph!* uttered to imitate a frog's croak, as the burden.

Mississippi. The peculiar sound is made in the same manner as that described in No. 17 above, but with an additional imitation of the quack of a duck. Following is the musical score for the last two lines of the stanza:

1 Mr. Frog went a-courting, an' he did ride,
   Och-kungh!
   Mr. Frog went a-courting, an' he did ride,
   A sword and a pistol by his side,
   Och-kungh, och-kungh, an' a quack! quack! quack!
   Och-kungh, och-kungh, an' a quack! quack! quack!

2 The first to come in was Mr. Fly,
   And he brought with him a pudding and pie.

3 The next to come in was Mistress Flea,
   And she brought with her a black-eyed pea.

4 The next to come in was Mr. Goose,
   And he took his fiddle and he cut loose.

5 There's bread and cheese upon the shelf,
   And if you want any just help yourself.

6 As they were crossing a big red lake,
   They all got swallowed by a big black snake.

(19) No. 19 is a dramatized version as sung by the late Dr. Kemp P. Battle, formerly president of the University of North Carolina. His custom was to gather a group of children about him and sing the song with great gusto and with improvised dramatic interpretations to suit the action.

1 Frog went a-courting, he did ride,
   Uhm-huhm;
   Frog went a-courting, he did ride,
   Sword and pistol by his side,   (Jump up and
   Uhm-huhm.   down as if rid-
                                        ing.)

2 He rode to Mistress Mouse's hall,
   Knocked at the door and loudly called.   (Knock on door
                                             and call.)

3 "Miss Mousie, are you within?"
   "O yes, kind sir, I sit and spin."

4   He took Miss Mousie on his knee,   (Take one of
    "Miss Mousie, will you marry me?"   children on knee.)

5   "Oh, no, kind sir, I can't say that,
    Without the consent of Uncle Rat."

6   Old Uncle Rat came a-riding home,   (Imitate riding,
    "Who's been here since I've been gone?"   Imitate voice of
                                                    rat.)

7   "A very fine gentleman has been here,   (Imitate voice
    Who says he'll marry me if you don't care."   of mouse.)

8   Old Uncle Rat laughed till he shook his fat side,
    To think his niece would be a bride.   (Laugh.)

9   Where shall the wedding supper be?   (Point far
    Way down yonder in the old hollow tree.   away.)

10 What shall we have for the wedding supper?
    Black-eyed peas and bread and butter.

11 First came in was Captain Bed Bug,
    And swore by all he had a rum jug.

12 Next came in was Colonel Flea,   (Dance with
    And danced the jig with the bumblebee.   one of children.)

13 The next to appear was old Sis Cow,   (Guests impro-
    Who tried to dance but didn't know how.   vised and imitated
                                                    ad libitum.)

14 And while they all were eating supper,   (Great confu-
    In came the cat and made a great splutter.   sion; children
                                                    scatter pell-mell.)

15 The first she pursued was old Uncle Rat,   (Run after and
    Knocked him down and spoiled his fat.   strike down a
                                                    child, gently.)

16 The next she pursued was Miss Mousie,
    But she ran up a hollow tree.

17 The frog he swam across the lake,   (Imitate swim-
    And got swallowed up by a big black snake.   ming.)

18 And this is the end of one, two, three,   (Count on fin-
    Frog and rat and Miss Mousie.   gers, beginning
                                                    with thumb on
                                                    o n e, throughout
                                                    last stanza, end-
                                                    ing on thumb on
                                                    the word *Mousie.*)

(20)   Another semi-dramatic version was supplied by Miss
Rosalie Jameson of Granger, formerly of Waco. Her family

came from Missouri about the middle of the nineteenth century and settled near Waco. Miss Jameson learned the song from her old white-haired negro mammy named Mary. At sleepy-time the old negro would take the child and sing the frog song with dramatic sounds or gestures, such as a cluck or a knock; and at the close when the child was asleep, the old mammy would kiss her lightly three times before putting her to bed.

1 Mr. Froggy went a-courtin', and a-he did ride,
   Uhm-huhm;
   Mr. Froggy went a-courtin', and a-he did ride,
   With a sword and a pistol by his side,
   Giddy-ap, giddy-ap (CLUCK, CLUCK, CLUCK) *giddy-ap.*

2 He rode up to Miss Mousie's hall,
   And there he made a great long call,
   Howdy-do, howdy-do (KNOCK, KNOCK, KNOCK) *howdy-do.*

3 He took Miss Mousie on his knee,
   And he said, "Miss Mousie, will you marry me?"
   Ple-ease do, ple-ease do (PLEASE, PLEASE, PLEASE) *ple-ease do.*

4 Oh, where shall the wedding be?
   Away down yonder in a holler tree;
   Lawdy-lawd, Lawdy-lawd (LAWD, LAWD, LAWD) *Lawdy-lawd.*

5 The first to come was a big black snake,
   And he made Mr. Froggy jump in the lake,
   Splinkity-splash, splinkity-splash (GLUB, GLUB, GLUB)
   splinkity-splash.

6 The next to come was a big black cat,
   And he made Miss Mousie fly the track,
   Bookity-book, bookity-book (BOOK, BOOK, BOOK) *bookity-book.*

7 . . . . shelf,
   And if you want to know any more, just sing it yo-self,
   Bye-ee bayby-eee (KISS, KISS, KISS) *bye-ee baby-eee.*

Versions of this E type, with the *uhn-huhn* burden, that I have in manuscript are listed below with the names of my informants.

(21) Mrs. James M. Harris, Austin; learned in Greenville, S. C., about 1880; seven stanzas.

(22) Miss Annie Ray Kieffer, San Angelo; learned from black mammy in Americus, Ga., about 1903; five stanzas.

(23) Miss Judith Porter, Dallas; traced back to tidewater counties of Mississippi and originally from Virginia; thirteen stanzas.

(24) Miss Hassie Davis, Haskell; learned in Robertson County about 1904; probably brought to Texas from Alabama; thirteen stanzas.

(25) Mrs. George L. Seay, Sheffield, Alabama; collected by my sister, Mrs. C. T. Morris; widely known in Alabama in the sixties; seventeen stanzas.

(26) Miss E. Lee Hartman, Trivoli, Refugio County; learned in De Witt County about 1906; said to have been brought over from New Orleans by her grandmother, and ultimately from Ireland by her great-grandmother; thirteen stanzas.

(27) Miss Ethel Burch, Austin; learned from her father, who came from Nashville, Tennessee, to Texas, about 1880; twelve stanzas.

(28) T. I. Briggs, Medina; learned from his father, who was of Scotch lineage; probably originally brought over directly from Scotland; sixteen stanzas.

(29) Miss Eleanor K. Taylor, Houston; learned from a grand-aunt in Cleveland, Ohio, and probably originally from Massachusetts; fourteen stanzas.

(30) Miss Joe Talley; learned from black mammy in Holly Springs, Mississippi, about 1900; fourteen stanzas.

(31) Miss Corinne Clark, through Miss Kathleen Crisman, both of Dallas; learned from grandmother, daughter of a Kentucky planter and slave owner; nine stanzas.

(32) From *Houston Chronicle*, supplied by J. C. Bridgewater, Chocolate Bayou; date of publication not given; thirteen stanzas.

(33) Mrs. J. H. Woolford, Austin, with assistance of her daughter-in-law, Mrs. A. L. Woolford; learned in Virginia seventy years ago; thirteen stanzas.

(34) Mrs. R. H. Baker, Austin; learned from her mother, Mrs. J. S. Faulkner, who came to Texas from Kentucky before the Civil War; ten stanzas.

(35) Mrs. J. C. Marshall, Quanah; learned in Arkansas about 1890; twelve stanzas.

(36) Mrs. Hawes Campbell, Enfield, King William County, Virginia; seventeen stanzas. (Referred to in No. 9 above, p. 27n.)

(37) From *Nashville Banner*, date not given; supplied by S. M. Young, Dixon Springs, Texas; twelve stanzas.

(38) Professor C. M. Montgomery, Austin; taken down from his mother-in-law, Mrs. M. W. Stanford, Waco, originally from Arkansas; six stanzas.

(39 *a* and *b*) Miss Edna McCormick, San Marcos, and her mother, Mrs. W. L. McCormick, Denton, Texas; learned by Mrs. McCormick from a negro house-servant brought by her parents from North Carolina in 1860; burden seems to imitate sound of frog; see (17) above; eight stanzas each.

(40) Mrs. R. T. Pritchett, of Corpus Christi, reports this version

as having been in her family for at least a hundred years. The family went first to North Georgia, near Atlanta, and then to Haynesville, Louisiana. Mrs. Pritchett learned the song in Louisiana and brought it with her to Texas. The method of singing the song is for the singer to take a child on the knees, and sway the knees gently until the chorus is reached. At the words *Ump! Humph!* the singer jogs or stops suddenly and thus dislodges the child from his knees. The words of the burden were written in imitation of a frog's croak. (Referred to on p. 40n. above.)

F.   (41)   Finally, in the F type I have found one negro version, that is, a version with a distinctive tune which has been handed down in a negro family for at least one generation.   Bessie Lee Thompson, the colored cook in a sorority house in Austin, says that she learned the song from her "daddy," Wesley Harris, at Bastrop, Texas, some twenty-five years ago.   Wesley claimed that he learned the song from a little white girl named Frances, when he was a small boy in his white folks' house at Elgin, Texas.   The tune is a characteristic negro melody, and varies now and then with the mood of the singer.   The burden changes from stanza to stanza, alternating between *daada daa, teedee dee, tedee dum,* and the like.   The words, too, are sometimes telescoped or rearranged. Bessie rarely sings the song over twice in the same way, and it was exceedingly difficult to get her version down in a semblance of order.   She says you can repeat a line or a part of a line at any point in the music to produce what she calls a "nachul tune."   I give the melody as nearly as possible as I learned it from Bessie.

1   Froggie went a-coat'n an' er-he did ride,
    Tadee daada daada daa,

Froggie went a-coat'n, and er-he did ride,
 Tadee daada daada daa.
Froggie went a-coat'n, an' er-he did ride,
Wid a s-word an' a pistol to his side,
 Tadee daadee deedaa daa,
 'Tadee daada dadee dum.

2 He went by Miss Mousie's house, (3 times as above)
 Miss Mousie she come a-friskin' out.

3 He taken Miss Mousie on his knee, (3 times)
 Ask her, "Dear, kin' Miss, will you have me?"

4 She said "Yaas, but where will de wedd'n be?
 Tadee daada daada daada daa,
 Where will de wedd'n supper be?
 Tadaa dedaa deeda dee,
 Where will de wedd'n supper be?"
 He said, "Way down yonder in a holler tree."
 Tadee dadee dadee dee,
 Tadee dedee dee dee.

5 She said, "What will de wedd'n supper be? (3 times)
 He said, "Two blue beans an' a black-eyed pea."

6 Fust come in wuz de bumblebee-e (3 times)
 A-pickin' de banjo on his knee-e.

7 Nex' come in wuz de Lady Flea; (3 times)
 She taken her seat in de holler tree.

8 Nex' come in wuz Mister Tick; (3 times)
 He et so much twel it made him sick.

9 Nex' come in wuz Doctor Fly; (3 times)
 Says, "Now, by George, dis tick mus' die."
 Tadee daada daadee daa,
 Daada deeda daa die.[19]

---

[19]Professor Thomas W. Talley, of Fisk University, prints in *Negro
Folk Rhymes* (1922) a negro dialect version of twenty-five stanzas,
giving the common tune with the *uhn-huhn* burden. Talley's version
seems to be a sort of composite dialect version made up by some fairly
skilful compiler. He also gives on p. 667 of his book a fragment which
he calls "Frog in a Mill (Guinea or Ebo Rhyme)." This appears to be
a conglomerate negroized fragment of the several *kimo-karo* nonsense
burdens. It may be worth recording here for comparison with the C type
burdens given above.

 Once dere wuz er frog lived in er mill,
 He had er raker don la bottom o' la kimebo
 Kimebo, nayro, fomididdle, all-a-board la rake;
 Wid er raker don la bottom o' la kimebo.

Practically all of the Texas versions are traceable to the older states, mainly the Southern States, Georgia, Alabama, South Carolina, North Carolina, Virginia, Tennessee, Arkansas, Louisiana, Mississippi, Missouri; one comes from New York *via* Connecticut; one from Massachusetts *via* Ohio; one comes from Maine, and another from Illinois; one is thought to be from Scotland, and another from Ireland. Most of the versions have the tragic ending of *one, two, three,* with *a big black snake* as the villain who swallows them up. Three or four of my versions show the additional fate of the snake about as follows:

> The big black snake it crawled upon the land,
> And it was killed by a backwoods man.
>
> The backwoods man he went to France,
> And that's the end of my romance.

The *backwoods man* becomes *a big French man* and *a big nigger man* in the other versions with this ending. One of these and three or four other versions add varying forms of the traditional conclusion,

> The knife and fork are on the shelf,
> If you want any more, just sing it yourself,

the *knife and fork* being sometimes displaced by the *saddle and bridle,* the *old hymn book,* and so forth. Two versions have the Ritson-Halliwell ending, "And that's the end of my history (old song) book." Several of the versions are incomplete, stopping short with the wedding supper, and one (MS. 23) has a distinctly happy ending—

> So there they danced and were very gay,
> They danced until the break of day.

In all my versions, except one, the *well,* which was the starting point of the frog in the *Melismata* song, has disappeared, and the *mill,* the home of the mouse, appears in but two versions. The older and now bookish form "a-wooing ride" has given place to "a-courting ride" in all of my versions except two; and the now obsolete *buckler* has uniformly been replaced by *pistol* in all Texas versions except one.[20] The "Dicke our

---

[20]I also find *buckler* in the Kentucky version of Wyman and Brockway, referred to on p. 10.

Drake" of the *Melismata* has become simply the cat, the old gray cat, the big yellow cat, the old tomcat, etc. In one of the Texas versions (30) a ferocious gesture to frighten the children is indicated at the word *grabbed* in the stanza,

> Next came in was a big yellow cat,
> And *grabbed* Miss Mousie by the back.

That the song was sometimes sung with other and more elaborate dramatic accompaniments is indicated by the version supplied by Dr. W. J. Battle (see No. 19 above). The variations in the wedding guests are numerous. Among others that "next come in" are Major Tick, Colonel Flea, Miss Bee, the bumblebee, Captain Snake, Mrs. Cow, Miss Rabbit, Mrs. Moth, Dr. Fly, Squire Snail, Captain June Bug, the mole so black, the old gray goose, a square old louse, a big red bug, a betsy bug, a bed bug, and a tumble bug, which is, indeed, as the *Melismata* song concludes, "a goodly company, the divelt go with all."

A TEXAS BORDER BALLAD

By Mattie Austin Hatcher

In the common parlance of present day Texans, "the Border" is understood to be the Rio Grande and adjacent territory. So "A Texas Border Ballad" suggests songs sung by Mexican *vaqueros* and Texas cowboys concerning raids, deeds of outlaws, and other more or less tragic incidents characteristic of the Rio Grande region. But to Spanish Texas at the end of the eighteenth century, "the Border" designated the Sabine River and the disputed strip lying between Louisiana and Texas. Prior to 1803, when "Napoleon tossed Louisiana into the lap of the United States," the rivalry along this Franco-Spanish frontier was intense, expressing itself in over-reaching diplomacy and eager aggression on the one hand and sullen jealousy and suspicion on the other.

Toward the end of the eighteenth century there prevailed along the Texas-Louisiana frontier social and political conditions conducive to a vigorous folk literature. The inhabitants of Louisiana, for the most part French in blood and responsive to the stirrings of the Revolution in their mother country, had, by a turn of the wheel of fortune in Europe, found themselves under the stern reactionary rule of Spain. To the feeling of contempt that the New-World Frenchmen always felt for the Spanish don there was added the galling yoke of political subjugation, which they fondly imagined could be thrown off with ease if a concerted attempt were made. Under these conditions ballads were common and expressive.

One ballad, at least, embodying all the elements inherent in the situation and found in the most unlikely place, has been preserved. The Bexar Archives contain the record of a law suit (1795) brought by Bernardo Dortolant, captain of the mounted militia of Natchitoches, Louisiana, against one Domingo Prudhomme, a soldier of the said company, for *singing a French song* that threatened the plaintiff and insulted him and other residents of Natchitoches. According to the facts set forth in Dortolant's complaint, the ballad had the following origin:

Disguised as Indians, four Frenchmen waited patiently one

night until certain men and women of the opposing (Spanish)
party came out of the house of the commandant, Don Luis de
Blanc. Here the visitors had whiled away many pleasant hours
to the music of a violin in the hands of Andres Ramben. The
four Frenchmen fell upon the revellers, gave Ramben a good
beating, and completely demolished his violin by breaking it
over his head. The rest of the party managed to save their
skins by escaping into a nearby house. As the attack was
made at night, the criminals could not be identified. On the
following day, with characteristic French wit, the footpads
circulated the report that the *revenantes,* or "ghosts," had
been the perpetrators, and one of their number composed a
ballad to celebrate the victory.

Now, just before this outrage, Bernardo Dortolant had
secured permission from the commandant of Natchitoches
and the governor of Louisiana to go over to San Antonio de
Bexar to assure the authorities there that certain late dis-
turbances in Louisiana had been caused by the intrigues of
"Citizen Genet," who, with certain misguided Americans, had
planned to seize Louisiana and Florida for France. Dortolant
chanced to depart just in time to avoid the attack made upon
the violinist and his friends. His escape enraged the Frenchmen, who consoled themselves by declaring that they would
take revenge if he ever dared to show his face in Natchitoches
again. On his return trip, Dortolant learned at Nacogdoches
that it would be dangerous for him to proceed. He, therefore,
appealed to the military authorities for protection. In his
complaint he quoted the objectionable French ballad, gave a
Spanish translation thereof, and then added certain explanations as to its meaning.

First, to understand the song, said he, it must be explained
that in Natchitoches *revenantes* is used to designate "ghosts"
or "souls of the dead who have returned to this world," and is
applied to those who are not supporters of the Spanish cause.
The adherents of the French call their enemies "aristocrats";
i.e., partisans of the monarchical form of government. Con-
sequently, they reserve the title "democrats" or "lovers of the
republican cause" for the *revenantes.* Andres Ramben,
whom they had beaten, was in the song designated as the
"Wandering Jew" and the "flatterer." They called Don Fran-
cisco Bossier "the teacher of little things" because he taught

his brothers-in-law. Two men had followed him into the woods and attacked him but he had escaped. He was warned in the song that he would again see the "ghosts," evidently meaning that the next time he would not escape. The ballad makers also accused him of entering the home of the former priest of Natchitoches to spy on what was being done. They called Don José Arman a poor "bankrupt" because the misfortunes he had suffered had reduced him to poverty. They also characterized him as a "spy" and a "dirty scamp" because he did not belong to the party that was hostile to the Spanish rule and because he had lived in the Province of Texas for many years. Besides, his daughter had married the eldest son of the commandant of Natchitoches; thus the threat that he would soon know quite well how to "receive the blows of the ghosts." They described the merchant, Don José Tozin, as "sorrel" because he was red like a sorrel horse. His wife was with Ramben and his party and, because Tozin was at home sick with a ring-worm, they threatened "to cure him quite suddenly." They called Pedro José Maz "the scullion of the bar-room"—meaning the boy who measured the drinks— because he was the man who surveyed the lands at Natchitoches. They, therefore, threatened to measure his shoulders.

They called Dortolant "the chief spy" because he was the acting commander-general at Natchitoches when the insubordination began. Then, as he was on the road to Bexar when the attack was made, the singers declared that he was "fleeing from the hurricane" and that he would make a long journey. As he was captain of the mounted militia of Natchitoches, they declared that they would "beat him with cords" when he returned and that they would "brush his shoulders." In the stanza beginning, "Puffed up with false position," they clearly and undeniably referred to the commandant of Natchitoches, for who could threaten to punish them save one in authority over them? Because he was compelled by the weakness of his military force to affect ignorance of the insurrection, they declared that he who had formerly treated them cruelly was now become lenient. The lines declaring that peace would perhaps follow in case the commandant did not "traitorously attack the souls of the dead who have returned to this world" meant that they would forgive him if he did not report them to the governor.

To understand the verses concerning Sardanapalus, said Dortolant, one must recall that Sardanapalus was the king of Persia and that, when he saw the enemy approaching his capital he retired to a fort with his wives and gave himself over to dancing and drinking. The implication could mean nothing else than that the commandant did not come out of his house at the beginning of the fight at Natchitoches but remained within in safety with his family. By the words, "Friend, you understand the sign," the ballad makers meant to say that he had better surrender himself unless he wished his house burned down over his head. In the last stanza the Frenchmen sang of the parish priest of Natchitoches, who had fled from France after the Revolution so as to be able to follow his faith freely. The expression, "He has poorly served the French chapel," merely indicated the strong leaning of the singers towards the French Revolution and their disaffection towards the Spanish cause, since they considered it a crime for the priest "to have fled from the doctrines of the Revolution."

With these explanations the French version and the Spanish translation as rendered by Dortolant will be intelligible, and the rhythmic English translation by Mr. Donald Lee Joseph, University of Texas, will be understood by a still wider circle of readers.

Mesieurs Ecouter un histhoire
Dont on nous farcit lamemoire
   Etant enfant
la chose est pourtant bien Certaine
Soufrez que lon Vous Entretiene
   des revenant

Les esprist St Voyant le trouble
que des Coeurs et des ames doubles
   Cause anosgens
Sont decendu Sur la terre
Pour Venger lhonneur De leurs freres
   en revenant

ils acosta dabord un homme
que lepublic icy surnome
   le juif errant
frere recoit la discipline
et plies humblement ton Echine
   Aux revenant

ausytot on le deculote
on luy touche une matellote
   en le faisant [fessant?]
le flateur veut fuir et secrie
mais polimant il remercie
   les revenant

Oigan Señores una historia
De la qe. nos llenaron la memoria,
Siendo niños.
La cosa es por tanto mui cierta.
Permitan Vmds.. qe. les hable
De las Almas de los difuntos que han
Buelto á este Mundo.

Estos Santos Espiritus viendo los enrre-.
   dos,
Que ciertos corazones y almas dobles,
Causan á nrâs. gentes.
Han vaxado sobre la tierra,
Para vengar el honor de sus herm[ano]s
Como almas de difuntos que han
Buelto á este Mundo.

Se acercaron luego á un
Aquien el Publico apellida.
El Judio andante.
Hermano recive la diciplina
Y dobla humildemte. tu ravadilla
A las almas de los difuntos que
Buelben á este Mundo.

Al instante levaxan los calz[one]s
Y le tocan una Marinera.
Azotandole.
El Soplon quiere huir y grita
Pero atentamte. da las gracias
A las almas de los difuntos qe. han
Buelto á este Mundo.

Un Falso tutor de menor que
Que no há entrado en la Casa Presbiterial
Que pa. ver lo qe. en ella se hacia.
Si el cree escaparse de la vengansa
El bolbera á ver vien pronto segun creo
Las almas de los difuntos qe. han
Buelto á este Mundo.

Vil Benqueroutier tu nous joue
espion flateur ame deboue
    detous les temp
tu scaura bientot lamaniere
dont on recoit les Etrivierre
    des revenant

Vil Bancarrotero tu nos juegas
Espia Soplona alma de lodo
De todos tpos.
Tu sabras bien pronto el modo
Como se reciven los azotes
De las almas de los difuntos qe. han
Buelto á este Mundo.

Sans onguant ny creme detarte
lon veut faire paser la derte
    a L'alesant
    [à l'alezan?]
ne Vaudront jamais les lianes
    des revenant

Sin inguento, ni crema de tartaro
Hacemos pasar el empeiñe al
Alasan
Las Pildoras ni las tisanas.
No valdran jamas las baras
De las almas de los difuntos qe. han
Buelto á este Mundo.

un Certain Comi de Cambuse
Se croyant lesprist de meduse
    Vil insollant
qui malgres nous toise nos **terres**
il te toiseron tes Echiniere
    les revenant

Un cierto Moso de Bodigon
Que cre tener la ciencia de Medusa
Vil insolente.
Que apesar nro. mide nras. tierras.
Te mediran tus espaldas
Las almas de los difuntos qe. han
Buelto á este Mundo.

le premier mouchar [moucheur *or* mou-
    chard?] fuit lorage
en partant en Pelerinage
    Pour quelques temp
mes les Verge sont toutes pretes
nous te broseront [battre?] tes Epaulletes
    en revenant

El primer espabilador hulle la tempestad.
Yendose en peregrinaje
Por algun tiempo
Pero las varas estan listas
Nosotros sepillaremos
Tus alamares
Quando buelvas.

Enivres de fause noblese
toy qui nous menase ou Carrese
    Selon les temp
Pelerin dis moy jeten prie
Situne Crains pas lafolie
    des revenant

Ensoberbesido de falsa nobleza
Tu que nos amenasas ó nos acaricias
Segun los tiempos
Peregrino de mí te suplico
Si tu no temes la locura de las
Almas de los difuntos que han
Buelto á este Mundo.

Consolle toy mon Cher Confrerre
tu nauras pas les Etrivierre
    dan Cemoment
lapaix succedera peut ettre
Sy tu nataque pas en traitte
    les revenant

Consuelate querido cofrade
Que no reciviras azotes
Por ahora
La paz sucedera puede ser
Si tu no atacas traicioneramente
Las almas de los difuntos que han
Buelto á este Mundo.

jadis le roy Sardanapal
dansait la ronde dans sa Salle
    enpresidant
Parmy sa cohorte de fammes
il feut Eclaire par les flames
    des revenant

En otros tpos. el rey Sardanapalo
Bailava la rueda en su sala
Como Presidente
Entre su Coorte de Mugeres,
El fue alumbrado pr. las llamas.
De las almas de los difuntos qe. han
Buelto á este Mundo.

tel feut la cruelle Vengeance
queprouva le Chef d ela danse
    de loriant
amy vous Comprenez lenblême
rendez vous au pouvoir supréme
    des revenant

Tal fue la cruel venganza.
Que esperimento el Gefe de la dansa
Del Oriente.
Amigo vos compreendeis el emblema
Rendios al poder Supremo.
De las almas de los difuntos qe. han
Buelto á este Mundo.

un Emígré de la rochelle
ayant mal Servy la chapelle
    du puple franc
il est party desonpayi
est [et?] commence a craindre la follie
    des revenant

Un emigrado de la Rochela qe. ha
Mal serv[i]do la Capilla
Del Pueblo franco.
Salio de su tierra
Y principio a temer la locura
De las almas de los difuntos qe. han
Buelto á este Mundo.

Gentlemen, listen to the story
With which our memories were filled
While we were children.
The thing is none the less true;
Let us tell you
Of the ghosts.

The holy spirits, seeing the trouble
That double-dealing hearts and souls
Cause our people,
Came down upon the earth
To avenge the honor of their brothers
As ghosts.

They first accosted a man
Whom people here know as
The Wandering Jew.
Brother, accept the punishment
And humbly bend your back
To the ghosts.

They quickly remove his trousers
And play for him a *Marinera*[1]
While they whip him.
The flatterer wants to escape and cries out,
But politely does he thank
The ghosts.

Low bankrupt, with us you are playing,
Flattering spy, dirty soul,
Forever.
You will soon know how
To take the strappings
Of the ghosts.

With neither unguent nor cream of tartar
They want to cure this sorrel fellow
Of the ring-worm.
Neither pills nor medicinal teas
Will be so effective as the thongs
Of the ghosts.

Oh, mister scullion from the bar-room,
Thinking yourself as wise as Medusa,
Insolent fellow,
Who measure our lands against our wills,
The measure of your shoulders will be taken
By the ghosts.

[1] A popular dance in Peru, Chile, and Ecuador.

The chief spy flees from the hurricane,
By departing on a pilgrimage
For some time,
But the cords are all ready.
We shall beat your shoulders for you
When you return.

Puffed up with false position,
You, who threaten or wheedle,
Depending on the need,
Pilgrim, tell me, I beg you,
If you aren't afraid of the rage
Of the ghosts.

Console yourself, my dear fellow;
You will not be whipped
At this moment.
A respite perhaps will follow
If you do not traitorously attack
The ghosts.

In times past the king Sardanapalus
Danced the rounds in his hall
As the master
Among his cohort of wives.
He was lighted by the flames
From the ghosts.

Such was the cruel vengeance
That overtook the chief
Of the Oriental dance.
Friend, you understand the sign;
Surrender yourself to the supreme power
Of the ghosts.

An emigrant from La Rochelle,
Having badly served the church
Of the French,
Quitted the shores of his country
And now begins to fear the madness
Of the ghosts.

REPTILES OF THE SOUTH AND SOUTHWEST IN FOLK-LORE

By John K. Strecker

In the *Publications* of the Texas Folk-Lore Society for 1925 I catalogued some Louisiana reptile myths, many of which are common to Texas, particularly East Texas. In the present contribution, I am bringing together a number of tales gathered on my rambles through the states of Arkansas, Louisiana, and Texas. The majority of these are of negro origin, some from the cypress swamps and bayous, others from as far west as the Brazos Valley. A few are West Texan, and still others owe their dispersion in this country to the influence of the early Scotch-Irish settlers of the Old South. I am attempting to treat these tales sympathetically, not as a naturalist but as a folk-lorist. In the course of time I hope to record practically all of the folk tales, both native and imported, relating to North American reptiles and amphibians. During the past year, I have spent considerable time studying the ways and beliefs of black-folk, descendants of African tribesmen, untainted by alien blood. Wherever they reside away from the changing influences of cities and large towns, these folk are a never-ending source of interest to the sociologist. In the valleys of the Red River of Louisiana and the Sabine River of Louisiana and Texas, are to be found negroes who use many African words, the inheritance of their ancestors. A white man is a "buckra," which word is used on the Calabar coast of Africa to indicate a demon—a superior being. A ground-nut (peanut) is a "pinda," and "niam" (nēam) means "to eat." When a negro mother whips her child, she gives it an extra lick for "brawtus," and in a trade something is sometimes thrown in for "brawtus," the word evidently having the same meaning as the Creole "lagniappe" or the Mexican "pilón." The customs and beliefs of these negroes are as marked as their language. If a heavy cloud appears at a time when rain is not desirable, an axe is struck in the ground to "split the cloud." A funeral is always a public affair. Most of the negroes within a radius of twenty miles attend and all sit up with the body of the deceased, even though, as Polly the cook expressed it, "she wa'n't acquainted wid de corpse." The vernacular word "varmint" (vermin) is used in a very broad sense. There are two classes of varmints: ordinary ones which may appear in the full light of day, and "varmints what move aroun' in de night," the latter class including "hants" (ghosts), foxes, raccoons, wildcats, opossums, and skunks.

How impotent would the up-to-date white physician who deals with the germ theory and operates for the relief of pain feel in the presence of Panora, who relieves the "misery" in her back by putting turpentine on a string and tying the string around her leg! And Panora explains that when you shiver, it is a sign that a rabbit is running over your grave. In the moonlight, you stroll down a "tote" road (a narrow foot-path) and you hear the melancholy cry of a night bird. You in-stinctively murmur "chuck-will's-widow"—and smile when your negro guide says, "Dat bird he say 'chip dropped out o' de white oak.' " And then it occurs to you that this bird be-longs to an avian family whose book name is "goatsucker," on account of a white man's myth implicitly believed in many por-tions of Europe, and for which no scientist has as yet been able to coin a better English name. The folk-lore of these black people is overflowing with accounts of many different kinds of animals; but by far the greatest number of supersti-tions are about reptiles and amphibians, because these are most feared.

It often is a difficult matter to separate folk tales told by whites from plain lies, especially when the relators are more or less sophisticated from having lived in thickly settled com-munities. With the breaking up of the great cattle ranges and the moving on of the cow-puncher, it has become almost an impossibility to gather the traditions of the cattle country in the freshness of their early form; they are now distorted and changed beyond measure. The collector of negro lore is on surer ground.

THE SNAKE DOCTOR

Have you ever seen a "snake doctor," one of those beautiful green or purple or maroon bodied creatures with filmy wings, which flit around marshes and lagoons, and which white men call dragon-flies? You may have commented on the beautiful iridescence of their coloring but, unless you were reared among the negroes of the Old South, you probably know nothing of their marvelous habits. You walk along the edge of a bayou and turn over a section of a dead cypress stump and find "old marse stump-tail moccasin" taking his afternoon nap. You dislodge him from his comfortable quarters and hit him a terrific blow on the head with a heavy stick and go on your way rejoicing that one more poisonous snake has been disposed of. But any thorough-going old-time swamp negro knows that he has not been disposed of. A moment after you leave the neighborhood of the moccasin, a beautiful insect—the "snake doctor"—alights on the head of the still squirming serpent. It gently and soothingly raises and lowers its transparent wings, accompanying this action by a peculiar movement of the head. In the course of a few minutes, the stump-tail shows signs of life, the wounds made by your bludgeon quickly heal, and soon he squirms to the edge of the water and disappears beneath its surface. The "snake doctor" gently flys along your path ready to give first aid should another snake require his ministrations. Remember this: *Unless you cut off a snake's head, a "snake doctor" can bring it back to life, even though its body may have been badly mutilated.*

THE STINK POT

The "stink pot" is a small turtle common to Southern streams. It seldom attains a length of more than four or five inches. Some men who claim to be versed in natural history call him the musk turtle. He bears a rather unsavory reputation due to his mephitine odor. An old negro in the swamps of Liberty County, Texas, thus explained the cause of his musky smell: "Yer see he lives in de mud neah whah Misser Polecat he come down ter drink. Stink pot he got no bettah sense en to try bite Misser Polecat an Misser Polecat sho make him smelly."

THE SNAPPER

The snapper is a large fresh-water turtle called "loggerhead," although this vernacular name really belongs to a salt-water species of much larger proportions. The snapper has an unusually large head, a very long neck, and the longest tail of any North American turtle with the exception of the alligator snapper, which is a much larger animal. On account of the small size of the snapper's shell, he is unable to protect himself by withdrawing into it and must fight for his life in the open. As a result, he is exceedingly vicious. A large specimen can very readily damage a person with its heavy jaws, even to the extent of amputating a finger or toe. You are advised by the negroes to "keep way from ole logger-head. Ef he bite you, he hole on tell it rain. Ef you kill him, he won die tell de sun go down."

THE KING OF THE SWAMP

In many lowland localities in the South, the negro story of the "king of the swamp" is still current. According to this story, the "king" is a large moccasin, not the ordinary stump-tail but a much larger creature. He attains a length of from ten to twelve feet and his body is as large around as a man's thigh. His home is usually the heart of a large, hollow cypress stump and here he holds forth for generations. He not only preys on large fish and an occasional water-fowl, but is very fond of eating other snakes, even other moccasins. Whenever there is a scarcity of other snakes, the negro fishermen attribute this to the depredations of the "king," who is supposed to be jealous lest some other serpent may increase to such proportions as to be able to contest for his domain. A negro once attributed the swollen condition of the corpse of a young boy who had drowned in a cypress swamp to his having "fust been bitten by de king moccasin."

"PISONOUS"

Negroes are noted for their use of peculiar (and sometimes apt) expressions. One commonly heard with reference to some odd-appearing but harmless amphibian or reptile is that "it looks pisonous." This expression "stumped" me for some time until I suddenly understood that the negro was trying to convey the idea that the appearance of the animal was remarkable and out of the ordinary. Black people have some strange ideas about the power of reptile venom. You are told not to kill a hoop or stinging snake with a stick, "because de pison run up yo arm an kill you." Should you catch a "lamper eel" on a hook and afterwards eat a fish caught on the same hook, you will be poisoned.

ANOTHER COACHWHIP STORY[1]

After a coachwhip "flagellates" you (his technical name is *flagellum!*) into an unconscious state, he will run his tongue up your nostrils in order to find out whether you are still alive. If you are, he will continue the whipping process until life becomes extinct. In some localities the whipping produces only unconsciousness, never death. In others, the poisonous element enters into the story, and the snake poisons his victim with each blow of his quirt-like tail.

TOADS

If you handle a toad, you will get warts on your hands. An old story (used by Shakespeare in *As You Like It*, Act II, Scene I, lines 12–14) which found its way into the South through early English settlers is that a toad has a precious jewel in its head, the heavy cranial crests providing protection and a hiding place for it. Decoctions brewed from dried toads were as popular among early negro "conjure" doctors in the South as they were among European physicians during the Middle Ages.

THE CHAMELEON

The green lizard, or "chameleon," is a small slender southern lizard that seldom attains a length of over half a foot. Its usual color is light yellow-green, and the male has a throat pouch, or "dewlap," of a beautiful pinkish color. This "dewlap" is capable of expansion, and by means of it the lizard is able to make a most interesting and wonderful sexual display during the mating period. This species, although only distantly related to the true chameleons of the African continent, is able

---

[1] See "Reptile Myths in Northwestern Louisiana," *Publications* of the Texas Folk-Lore Society, No. IV (1925), page 50.—Editor.

to change its general coloration to a marked degree, these changes running through drab and several shades of brown to the most vivid green. To the imaginative negro of the South, who regards each reptile as a "bogey," is given the power to witness even more wonderful transformations. According to him, the lizard changes to every color of the rainbow and all the intermediate shades, but only under certain peculiar conditions (usually not mentioned). Questioning generally fails to elicit further information, but an old Uncle Remus of the swamps once suggested that there were many sights open to the eyes of the negro that were not given to white men to see!

"OLE RED-HEAD SCARPION"

The red-headed skink, or "scarpion," is common in the timbered regions of the South. Large specimens attain a total length of ten inches (head, body, and tail) and the head of an adult male will measure almost an inch across the temporal region. The adult skink usually lives in tall hollow trees, and the bottomland negroes believe that either its bite or sting will produce death. In the negro vernacular, scorpion, or "scarpion," means a poisonous animal. But the true scorpion is popularly called a "stinging lizard," this misnomer being in common use throughout the state of Texas. "Chillun, yo bettah keep way from ole red-head scarpion; yo go neah whah he is, he sho chase en sting yo. Ef he sting yo, yo sho gwine ter die."

SALAMANDERS, SPRING LIZARDS, AND GROUND PUPPIES

The salamander must have a body composed of asbestos—he cannot be burned but can live in fire. There is a difference, however, between the ancient mythical salamander, which was an enormous creature of remarkable appearance, and the small amphibious animal to which the miraculous property has been transferred by moderns. The "spring lizard" is a small aquatic or semi-aquatic salamander which inhabits springs or the vicinity of them. These tiny animals are abundant in Western Europe and the Eastern United States. Many of the folktales concerning "spring lizards" that are at present in circulation in the South are of very ancient lineage. They were brought from the north of Ireland at the time the Scotch-Irish settled the hill counties of the states of Tennessee, Kentucky, the Virginias, North Carolina, and (Northern) Alabama, and were in time dispersed over the entire Southland. The following is undoubtedly of European origin, probably a Scotch "old wives' tale": "If you stick out your tongue and run it over the body of a spring lizard, you will be endowed with the spirit of prophecy." Here is an important recipe: "In case you swallow a spring lizard, you can rid yourself of it in the following manner: Eat two salt herrings and abstain from drinking water for half a day. Then lie down near the spring and the lizard will come out of you and go into the spring to drink." (This dates back to Europe in the Middle Ages and was brought into the South by the Scotch-Irish element of population.)

Ground, or mud, puppies[2] are land salamanders and the superstitions regarding these animals would alone fill a large volume. The following stories prove conclusively that conjurers and witch doctors and hoodoos are still at work among Southern negroes. You are told that if you will kill a ground puppy and dry its body and powder it and then place it in a small bag and conceal the bag under the doorstep of a house, the first person who crosses the threshold will receive into his veins the rejuvenated body of the ground puppy. A negro preacher admitted that he and two other negroes had assisted in releasing a ground puppy from the veins of a young girl. It was finally "cornered" in the girl's arm; and while one of the party pressed one end of the vein, another held hard at the other, and, although the ground puppy struggled back and forth, its release was effected by the use of a razor.

Mr. J. P. Simmons, of the English Department of Baylor University, who has studied the negroes of Northern Louisiana, very kindly furnishes the following: In some sections, a circlet of copper wire, to which is attached a dime as a charm, is worn around the ankle in order to prevent salamanders from getting into the body of the wearer. "White man, yo don believe hit but hit sho am true. When yo walks in de grass in yo bar feet, ef yo has cracks in yo feet, salamander sho gwine git in yo, less yo has dis chahm and den they cain't climb

---

[2]*Op. cit.*, page 51.—Editor.

ovah hit." A girl was suffering intense internal pain and a "conjure" doctor was called in. He took the girl into a private room and in a short time emerged triumphantly, holding aloft a bottle containing the body of a salamander which he had "conjured" out of the girl's arm.

THE HELLBENDER

The hellbender is a large aquatic salamander which is found in Western New York and the Great Lakes system, Iowa, and southward to Georgia and Louisiana.[3] It attains a maximum length of two feet and is much dreaded by fishermen, who consider it unlucky to catch one on a hook. In common with other large salamandriform amphibians, it is reported to be very poisonous. It is usually found in streams of clear, cool water. At Boiling Spring, Missouri, a negro fisherman very gravely told my friend, the late Julius Hurter, that the animal is called "hellbender" because it is one of the creatures that inhabit the infernal regions. Let us hope that he was not dispensing first-hand information!

THE GREAT WATER DOG OF THE PLAINS

In the plains region of Western Texas, the large tiger salamander is a common animal. During the dry season it lives below the surface of the ground in deserted prairie dog and ground squirrel burrows. After the first heavy rain of the year, it comes forth to breed in the shallow lakes that dot the surface of the plains. The adult animal has a broad, flat head, four well-developed limbs, a long tail, and a smooth, moist skin; and large specimens attain a maximum length of ten inches. Small specimens are sometimes called "lizards" by the natives, while large ones are called "alligators." This animal, in common with all salamanders, goes through a larval, or axolotl, stage of existence before finally attaining the adult form. These larvae have large, plump, light-colored bodies, external gills, finned tails, and large broad heads, and in general appearance look not unlike small catfish. In this stage, the animal has a voracious appetite and feeds upon

---

[3]Stejneger and Barbour, *Check List of North American Amphibians and Reptiles*, 1917, p. 7.

young spade-foot toads, toad tadpoles, grasshoppers, and other small creatures that either inhabit or accidentally fall into the lakes. The axolotl form is so different in appearance from the adult animal that it is usually given another name, that of "water-dog." According to some Texas cow-punchers, who somehow understand that the two forms are the same animal but do not understand the significance of the transformation, the tiger salamander is "one of the devil's brood; he can change from fish to lizard and then change back again!" He is considered a poisonous animal and classed with rattlesnakes, centipedes, tarantulas, and "vinagarones" (vinegarroons).

Along the New Mexican border is related a story of an enormous and extremely ferocious animal that formerly inhabited one of the salt lakes in Andrews County, Texas. It was an amphibious animal "resembling a great water-dog" and was said to feed almost exclusively on ducks and other water-fowl. It was said to make a terrific noise as it plowed its way through the water in the early morning, causing the ducks to arise in great flocks from the surface of the lake. It even put to hurried flight parties of gunners who became frightened at its ferocious appearance. A description of the animal given in a copy of a small plains newspaper of twenty-five years ago (unfortunately since lost) reminded one of the great prehistoric animals. The "great water-dog" has not been reported in recent years.

HORNED TOADS

If the strange and interesting horned lizard, or "toad," as it is called in the vernacular, were an inhabitant of the bayou counties of Louisiana and Eastern Texas, instead of the drier regions to the westward, where negroes are less imaginative, folklorists would have much more material to place on record. In the Brazos Valley, you are told that "when a horned toad spits blood from its eyes and then bites you, it is sure death." When a horned toad attacks a red ant bed in the spring, the "king of ants" sends out a scout to discover whether the invader is thin (just through hibernating). If he is, the "king" sends out his soldiers and they sting the toad to death. There may be a basis of truth to the story of the ants' getting the better of their gigantic enemy, for in early spring I have found horned toad bodies in proximity to ant beds, emaciated and partly-eaten. The animals may have been too weak to withstand repeated onslaughts of multitudes of attackers.

DON'T SWALLOW A LIZARD

Never permit a scaly lizard to climb your body, for if you open your mouth you are likely to swallow it and may never be able to rid yourself of it. Many persons have swallowed lizards, and within recent years old-time negro "conjure" doctors have used charms and formulas to rid the victims of their unwelcome body content. (Do not mistake a scaly lizard for a "spring lizard." It is the latter that you swallow when you drink at an open spring.)

THE GLADE DEVIL

The glade devil inhabits the Ozark Mountains of Missouri and Arkansas. It is a large lizard that sometimes grows to a length of sixteen inches, but specimens of this size are exceptional. Its general color is green or gray and its back is ornamented with white spots. The male has a double black collar and his head is unusually broad and vicious looking. The glade devil lives around and under flat stones in open woods and is noted for its prowess and ferocity. According to the stories, it is dangerous to invade the haunts of this creature, for it will chase a person even though he may be riding a horse and it can always outrun the horse. It bites with its teeth and stings with its tail and has a loud bark that can be heard for miles. In Middle and Western Texas, this creature is called a "mountain boomer." It is to be understood that the glade devil, or boomer, is poisonous.

WITCH SNAKES

A "witch snake" is a most peculiar creature. You will be unlucky all the days of your life if you happen to kill one. It is a blotched snake of rather small dimensions. The top of its

head is always ornamented by a picture of some kind. Sometimes it is a woman with long hair, again it is an old man
with pointed beard, and occasionally it is a human skull. This
story would have a much wider circulation if negroes were not
afraid to examine dead snakes, for according to my observations, all young chicken snakes *(coluber quadrivittatus)* are
witch snakes, and in most specimens the outlines of the
pictures are very distinct. If you don't believe that such
a thing as a witch snake exists, examine the head of a
young chicken snake from twelve to twenty-four inches in
length and see the picture for yourself. But be sure not to
kill the snake; you will suffer from some accident if you do.
In other words, a witch snake is a sure hoodoo. I first heard
the story of the witch snake from a negro octogenarian in
the Brazos Valley. I had captured a small chicken snake and
was examining it when the old darky stepped up. As soon
as he noticed the snake, he said, "Massa, dat's er witch snake.
Don kill et, er yo chillun die en yo cows give bloody milk, er
somethin happen ter yo." Since the head markings change
as the snake grows older, the negroes do not recognize the
adult as a witch.

SNAKES SWALLOW THEIR YOUNG

All snakes swallow their young. This has been known
for centuries but naturalists still refuse to give credence to
the story. Ask any old negro who lives in the woods and he
will tell you of some instance. If he didn't see the act himself, one of his uncles or his grandfather did. It generally
happens in this way. While in the woods, you suddenly come
upon a female snake and her brood sunning themselves. At
the first sound you make, the mother snake opens her mouth
and the young snakes immediately seek refuge in the body
of their parent. If you don't believe this story, kill the snake
and you will find the young ones inside her throat. The brood
may number a hundred or more, even if naturalists do claim
that a female snake seldom gives birth to more than thirty-
five young ones at one time. The following passage from
Spenser's *The Faerie Queene* (1590) should forever settle all
controversy as to the number of young produced by a single

female and prove the swallowing story beyond peradventure:

> A thousand yong ones, which she dayly fed,
> Sucking upon her poisnous dugs . . .
>
> . . . .
>
> Soone as that uncouth light upon them shone,
> Into her mouth they crept, and suddain all were gone.

This interesting story hails from no particular country or continent but seems to have sprung up spontaneously in all countries. Wherever snakes are found, this myth is current.

THE KING SNAKE

In some sections the beautiful coral snake (red, yellow, and black in accumulated bands) is called the king snake and is endowed with sufficient stinging ability to kill a live oak tree; in reality it is perfectly harmless. The king snake as denominated by scientists is a long, smooth, black fellow with white or yellow specks or splotches on his scales. He is as innocuous as the coral snake—but not so do the folk regard him. According to them, he is, indeed, "the king of all the snakes," lording it over all other serpent creation. If he takes a notion to disagree with one of his vassals, he ends the argument by killing and eating the other snake. He kills and eats rattlesnakes larger than himself. He kills them by repeated blows of his tail, crushes their bones, covers the shapeless mass with saliva, and then swallows it whole. No other snake can vanquish the king snake; he is vulnerable only to the attacks of man.

WHEN SNAKES GO BLIND

Of course, snakes do shed their skins, and while the slough is hardening and becoming dry and loose, snakes are not in good physical condition and are inclined to strike aimlessly. This fact has led to the popular belief that in late summer snakes go blind. Many folk will tell you that during the "dog days" the rattlesnake is blind. "Look out for er blin' snake," say the negroes. "He sho hev mo pison en when he kin see."

WHERE RATTLESNAKES DEN

Every particular locality in "rattlesnake country" has some favorite denning place where snakes retire for the winter. This is even granted to be more or less a fact by naturalists, but whether the den is merely a hibernating place for the local serpentine population or is a convening place for snakes from counties around has never been satisfactorily determined. At any rate, some marvelous tales have been told of the number of snakes in these dens. A favorite locality, so I am told, was formerly a place in Yellow Canyon, in the Uvalde country of Texas. Here rattlesnakes to the number of thousands, many of them ten feet in length and as big around as a man's thigh, gathered "back in the cattle days."

CONSTRICTORS

According to popular conception, nearly all large snakes are constrictors. A large constrictor will squeeze the body of its prey until all of its bones are broken and then with tongue lick the shapeless mass and swallow it whole. No matter how large the victim, its body is covered with saliva before the engulfing process begins. Though the rattlesnake is not credited with being a constrictor, he is supposed to use his tongue on victims intended for food. With respect to tongue and saliva, such conceptions are purely fabulous, and it is very questionable whether the constricting process of any snake does more than strangle the victim.

THE HAPPY FAMILY OF THE PLAINS

Out on the western plains, in the land of little rain and on its borders, lives, according to a fading popular belief, the most curiously assorted happy family in the world. There the prairie dog, the "prairie dog owl," and the rattlesnake all find home and companionship in the same burrow. Old time cow-punchers knew this to be a fact, but the prairie dogs and the scientists have always disagreed.

A PROTECTION AGAINST RATTLESNAKES

When you are camping in rattlesnake country, coil a horse-hair rope around your bed and no rattlesnake will cross it. A rattlesnake has been known to squirt his poison at his victim beyond the rope.

WHY IS A COAL OF FIRE DROPPED ON A LAND TERRAPIN'S SHELL?

In many sections of the South, it is a common practice among negroes to drop coals of fire on the shells of living box tortoises. In Florida, where the gopher turtle is a prized article of food, this act has a utilitarian urge, the object being to cause the animal to extend its head and neck so that it can be easily decapitated. In other sections, where the smaller land terrapins are treated in the same manner, the motive comes from sheer cruelty. In East Texas, however, I once heard an old darky call out to a land terrapin, "Go long dah less I put er cole on yo en mek yo move. Yo nevah gwine git home fo dark less yo move fasser." This made me wonder if the act had not some connection with a folk tale, but the negro refused to enlighten me.

ON THE ORIGINS OF REPTILE MYTHS

By John K. Strecker

During the past two years or more, I have spent much of my spare time studying folk beliefs concerning our Southern reptiles, and have tried to trace down their probable sources. This phase of study, if carried to its conclusion, might lead one into the depths of psychology, but such an investigation would in some degree eliminate the true folk, or primitive, interest. Therefore I shall attempt to hold my findings within more restricted bounds. It does not require a psychologist to tell us that almost every one of the grossly exaggerated and imaginative tales related by both white and black people owes its origin, at a far distant time, to an actual human experience. A simple but misunderstood incident often formed the nucleus that later developed into a marvelous tale of red eft or basilisk.

Egotism and boastfulness in man are responsible for the elaboration of some of our myths, but it is usually fear and superstition that originate them. Medicine men and conjurers in savage lands, through their use of dried snakes, lizards, and toads in both their professional equipment and their hut decorations, are responsible to a large extent for the fear these creatures inspire in the primitive minds of their tribesmen. The physician of the Middle Ages and earlier, with his grewsome "signs" hanging before his doors—skulls and stuffed snakes and clusters of dried toads—also had his influence in more civilized countries. If a decoction of dried toads was a panacea for ills, there must be something uncanny about the living animals themselves! A deliberate attempt to mystify "patients" has been a ruling passion among "medicine men" from the beginnings of history to the present time—from the magician and conjurer to the modern M.D. Dried headless lizards, toad broth, incantations, mystical word formulas and camouflage of technical terminology, all, in a way, belong in the same class. In Central Africa, it served the dusky medicine man's purpose to strike terror to the hearts of his tribesmen. So he instilled the belief in his

dupes that certain animals possessed not only human in-
stincts but god-like powers as well. The fang of the puff-
adder, the tooth of the crocodile, and the mummified body
of the chameleon were all connected in some way with the
fetichism of the natives and, through ignorance and superstition, endowed with magical powers.

Legends of a witch-doctor in the form of a crocodile are by
no means uncommon in Central Africa. My father, who spent
many years in the Old South before the Civil War, told me that
he once heard a Mississippi negro refer to an old bull 'gator as
"ole witch-doctor." This black man was no doubt the son
of a slave born in the Congo. Folk-tales about certain
reptiles originate, of course, in the countries in which these
animals live, *and if the same story is current in several countries it is an indication that somewhat similar animals live in
them.* If an imported folk tale is to live beyond a few generations, it must be applied to some specific creature in the new
land. Likewise, while some reptilian myths are local because
their subjects have a very limited distribution, others are
dispersed throughout an entire country. For example, the
blind cave salamander, *Typhlomolge rathbuni* (Stejneger), is
known from only one locality in the world, San Marcos, Hays
County, Texas, where a number of specimens came up in
the flow of water from an artesian well, and any wonder
tale concerning this amphibian would naturally have a very
limited circulation. On the other hand, the so-called "hoop
snake" ranges from Virginia to Florida and west to Texas,
and in the Mississippi Valley north to Indiana, and the story
of its reputed peculiarities is widely told. It is a great pity
that more negro lore was not gathered in ante-bellum days
when there were many slaves still fresh from the African
continent, for some of these stories might have shed light
on the origin of myths that, in diluted form, are still current
in the Southern States. The story of the friendship of the
serpent and the terrapin, which is still told in the backwoods of the Southeastern States, particularly in Alabama
and Florida, strongly resembles a similar tale related by one
of Henry M. Stanley's Basoko boys. In the Southern version,
the serpent proved his friendship for his terrapin relative
by killing a great blue heron ("blue crane" in the negro
vernacular) and thus avenging the death of the terrapin's

"child." In the African tale, which is quite long, the serpent kills queen (white) crane in order to avenge the death of the terrapin's mother, the terrapin having previously slain the crane's "old ma." In his efforts to get even, the terrapin seeks the advice of the jackal, the elephant, and other animals. The American version is simply the same story slightly distorted and shorn of its preliminary chapters.

Folk tales may thus be transferred from one country to another. Occasionally, through some confusion, they are transferred from one animal to another. In my catalogue of the amphibians and reptiles of Texas,[1] I refer to an Indian tradition that the alligator was once an inhabitant of Northwest Texas (the Panhandle) and that the animals were driven out of that section by a long-continued drouth, that they journeyed overland in immense droves, headed for the Gulf Coast, and that they never afterward returned. I have found interest in tracing the source of this tradition because I do not believe that the Mississippi alligator has been an inhabitant of the Panhandle within recent times. This great reptile selects as its haunts swamps and streams with wooded banks. The water courses of the northwestern counties are hardly suited to be the environment of more than a few species of fresh-water shells, and these such as are able to adapt themselves to unfavorable conditions and can for long periods exist in a state of hibernation. The Panhandle streams certainly were never suited to be the home of immense, active saurians. It is doubtful whether alligators have been found in the northwestern counties since the Pleistocene Age. However, the name *alligator,* a corruption of the Spanish *lagarto* (lizard), is frequently used in West Texas to indicate the large tiger salamander (or water-dog), which is abundant there. During long-continued drouths, these animals rarely come above ground but remain in their haunts deep down in deserted prairie dog and ground squirrel burrows. After heavy rains they come forth to procreate their species, the females depositing their eggs in the waters of rain-formed lakes. The fact that at such times these animals are present in great numbers, crawling along the trails and the flats between lakes, and then again are apparently absent for years,

[1]*Baylor University Bulletin*, Vol. XVIII, No. 4, August, 1915, pp. 1–82.

must have given rise among the Indians to the story of the great migration. Then, it would appear, early white settlers transferred this tradition of the plains "alligator" (the tiger salamander) to the Mississippi alligator. According to the Indian migration tradition, this particular drouth lasted for a period of more than seven years. It is just as easy for an Indian to be mistaken as it is for a white man.

Some of our foremost herpetologists persistently repeated a statement that the solitary spade-foot toad of the Eastern States, *Scaphiopus holbrooki* (Harlan), "mysteriously appeared in numbers, bred in abundance in ponds and ditches, and then disappeared, often for periods of years." The solitary spade-foot is both a burrowing and crepuscular beast and it breeds regularly every spring, but like most toads and frogs can be successfully hunted only in the early part of the night. Its "nocturne," the loudest made by any known species of amphibian, was probably credited to the bullfrog, and Eastern herpetologists for a long time continued to hope that they might some day "accidentally happen" to be present on the appearance of the spade-foot multitude. As a matter of fact, the animals were constantly present and were conducting their affairs with all of the regularity of good citizens. Having to relate this parallel story is a painful confession for a naturalist to make; but I must admit that our ignorance of the habits of most cold-blooded animals is so vast in its extent that we cannot always afford to severely criticize the unlettered when they fail to understand the ways of living creatures and attribute to them peculiarities and powers which they fall short of possessing. However, I shall be unwilling to admit that I have wrongfully traced the origin of my alligator story until some one produces a recent skeleton or skin of *Alligator mississippiensis* from the Canadian Valley of Texas!

As an illustration of how personal experience sometimes seems to confirm legendary belief, I can readily imagine a negro's slipping into a thicket and arousing a coachwhip snake from its *siesta*. I can almost see the whites of the negro's eyes and the grayish color of his skin as the startled reptile, in its efforts to escape, whisks between his legs. The negro runs—he almost flies—and at every leap and bound he fancies that vine and branch and sapling are but sections of the terrible

snake attempting to whip him in his hurried flight. He es-
capes—and becomes an additional witness in the slander case
against one of the most harmless and cowardly of snakes.
This example may seem an exaggeration; but a friend of mine,
an intelligent contractor, tells me that when he was a half-
grown boy, he once thought that he was pursued by a coachwhip and discovered only when he reached home, thoroughly
exhausted and out of breath, that he was being struck by
the old rope halter that he was carrying slung over his shoulder
and that he had forgotten.   (There is no copyright on this
story—I have since heard other versions of it!)

We are willing to admit that the "hant" story, told by some
person not related to us, has a logical explanation—that the
supposed ghost might have been the old white horse or an owl
hooting or something of the kind; but we protest when some
one claims that our Uncle Joe *did not* see a snake that sepa-
rated its body into a dozen sections and then later united the
fragments and crawled away, or that Grandpa *did not* see a
snake that rolled down the road like a hoop. We *know* that
neither Uncle Joe nor Grandpa would tell a lie and usually
ignore the possibilities that these relatives have been mistaken,
that their mental processes have been influenced by tales told
to them in the days of their youth, or even that they have taken
these old tales unconsciously for their own.

Circumstantial evidence is accountable for one of the most
widely extended of all folk beliefs about snakes. Miss Ratchford of the Wrenn Library, University of Texas, in an interesting letter to me, refers to an old poem which I had forgotten.
I quote her communication: "When I was a child I found in
some old recitation book a grewsome poem entitled 'The
Dukite Snake.' The story was something like this. A traveler killed a dukite snake and its mate followed him for a long
period of time and for a long distance, and at last took its
revenge by biting and killing the wife and children of the
traveler. I used to have dreams about

> . . . the terrible dukite snake
> That follows you like death or fate,
> And kills you sure as you killed his mate.

In a former article on reptile myths,[2] I incidentally refer

---

[2]*Publications* of the Texas Folk-Lore Society, No. IV, "Reptile Myths
in Northwestern Louisiana," pp. 44–52.

to the legend of the Australian tiger snake following the slayer of its mate, and speak of the similarity between this story and the negro superstition current in the Brazos Valley of Texas that the copperhead moccasin will wreak vengeance when any one kills its mate.   I am convinced that this is another cosmopolitan superstition of spontaneous growth.   I have even found traces of it in Oriental folk-lore, in which the avenger is a species of sand-viper.   The stories probably originated in each instance from the death of a native's wife or child by the bite of some poisonous reptile.   The husband or father, as the case might be, recalled having recently killed a similar reptile and at once concluded that the killing by the snake was an act of vengeance.   Poisonous serpents, especially the thick-set viperine species, are much more sluggish than the slender non-poisonous snakes and, as a rule, do not show so much disposition to make a hurried flight.   Therefore a *pair* of venomous snakes is much more likely to be seen or killed at the same time.   In turning logs in the river bottoms, not only in the mating season in early spring but in the late fall as well, it is a common thing to come upon an apparently mated pair of copperheads.   I have always found it a safe plan, when finding one copperhead, to look for the other.

Some superstitions have a practical basis.   For example, in West Texas, it is said that if one kills a horned toad, his mother's cows will either go dry or give bloody milk.   This is probably a "scare" story to prevent children from killing the valuable horned toad, which is a consumer of red ants and other injurious insects.   Horned toads are also said to spit poison when they are teased.   This belief has its foundation in the peculiar habit of this creature of ejecting fine streams of blood from the eyes when it is roughly handled.   The Brazos Valley negroes call this act "spitting blood," but the fluid seems to come from either a gland or ruptured blood vessel.   Those interested in the literature of this peculiar habit should consult Hay[3] and Stejneger[4] and a brief note by the present writer.[5]

[3]*Proceedings* U. S. National Museum, 1892, Vol. 15, pp. 375–378.

[4]U. S. Dept. Agric. Bureau Biological Survey, "North American Fauna," 1893, No. 7, pp. 159–228.

[5]*Proceedings* of the Biological Society, Wash., 1908, XXI, pp. 165–170.

It is easier to discover wonders in the moon or peculiarities
in the lives of animals we fear (these for cause being held
at long range) than it is to discover strange things about the
domestic animals that we daily feed or drive or pet.   Human
wonderment and fear of the unknown, as well as the alien
character of reptiles, are responsible for the extensive body
of superstition about them.   Only a few native birds figure
to any great extent in negro folk-lore.   It is true that the
jaybird is never seen on a Friday because he spends that day
carrying sticks to the devil in hell, that the owl is a bird
of ill-omen, and that several other birds have similar stories
related of them.   But in many localities where 200 or more
avian species are found during the course of the year, less than
a score belong to the dubious class.   Among reptiles and amphibians the case is quite different.   In my own locality, where
eighty-one species of these animals have been discovered, practically 80 per cent have poisonous and "conjure" properties
and are therefore shunned.

That accurate naturalist and clever writer, W. S. Blatchley,
of Indiana, in his little volume entitled *Gleanings from Nature,* includes one of the most interesting and valuable articles
on snakes that I have ever read.   Mr. Blatchley is material-
istic and does not appreciate legends.   He classifies all out-of-
the-ordinary snake beliefs as "lies" without trying to figure
out how they originated.   He speaks of many "lies" about the
blue racer, or blacksnake, and adds that all of these things are
deeds that no snake ever did or ever will do.   I grant that he
may be correct when he says that this species does not charm
birds or drink milk in milk houses or even suck cows but, like
the best of us, he in one instance overshoots his mark.   He
says that snakes do not steal eggs.   Now, almost any Texas
farmer boy can relate instances where the gray pilot or chicken
snake has entered his father's hen house and disposed of eggs.
In the Bayor University museum is the skeleton of a chicken
snake that came to its death on account of its inability to
distinguish the product of the hen from a china nest egg, and
the latter is still *in situ.*   Blatchley's explanation of what he
terms the "hoop snake lie" is that it is based on the ability of
a certain species of king snake to form its body into a loop,
much after the manner of a measuring worm.   This would
account for the shape that the "hoop" snake is supposed to

assume but not for the stinger; in fact, the animal he supposes to be the pseudo-hoop snake has no extension of the last caudal vertebra as has the Southern "stinging," or "hoop," snake. In an article referred to above,[6] I mention the stinging snake and its so-called stinger. It may be of some interest to folklorists to learn that it is now possible to explain the function of this instrument. The observations of Mr. Percy Viosca, of New Orleans, as well as my own, prove conclusively that the "stinging" snake uses this sharp caudal extension as a means of holding the slippery mud eel, or siren, on which he feeds, while he is working it in position to swallow.

[6]See Note 2, *ante*.

FAMILIAR SAYINGS OF OLD TIME TEXANS

By Mary Jourdan Atkinson

When Austin's colonists came to settle on the Brazos, they brought with them the varied idioms of the older states, many of which were ancient in Europe before Columbus first sighted the Bahama Islands. But language always takes color from its environment, and many of the sayings of the old world when brought to the new were gradually translated into figures expressive of American life. In the South and Southwest the work of men and women on the plantations and small farms, the business of riding over great ranges, of hunting Indians and game, of just living next to the ground with the implements of the soil in hand naturally brought to mind such comparisons as "sticking closer than a cocklebur" and "counting the chickens before they hatch."

As an example of a saying produced by local conditions, consider "plotting against the whites." This phrase, so suggestive of the danger and distress endured on Indian frontiers, is now never used in actual seriousness; but wherever a group has withdrawn for momentary conference, some friendly voice is sure to inquire: "Well, are you plotting against the whites?" And, like "How do you do?" the question is seldom answered. In Grimes County, Texas, a story similar in form to an Aesop fable is told concerning the origin of the expression, "He didn't say turkey to me." According to the Grimes County version, which has been furnished, with other material, by Mrs. L. N. Throop of Austin, an Indian and a white man went out hunting together. The net result of their day's scouting was a buzzard and a turkey. At parting, the white man offered to make a division of the game and the Indian assented. "Well," said the white man, "I'll give you your choice: you take the buzzard and I'll take the turkey, or I'll take the turkey and you take the buzzard." No matter which the Indian's choice, he was given the buzzard, and after some ruminations on the subject, he remarked to his friends: "He didn't say turkey to me one time." "Sweating like a nigger at election" is a commentary on Reconstruction days that every Southerner understands.

The sayings and similes that follow have been gathered mostly from the speech of native Texans, though many of them are current in other regions. Only a few of the more homely proverbs and maxims of the generation just passed are here included, though proverbs seemed to fall endlessly from their mouths, and they apparently thought that every word must point a moral, especially in the hearing of the young. They drew proverbs bodily or else paraphrased them from the Bible, Aesop's Fables, McGuffey's readers, and a few other books of household literature. As a consequence, the proverbs are generally lacking in the soil qualities so freshly apparent in many of the similes and other sayings.

As the old Scotch woman said of the ballads, many of the expressions here gathered together "were not made for reading." They are meant to be spoken. A term of derision as used by a Texan whose speech is still rich with folk sayings and native similes may have little meaning when only the actual words are considered, but the knowing tone and the twitch of the eyebrow that accompany the expression will make it comprehensible to the veriest stranger. Impossible, indeed, to look seriously upon a project after an old timer has said of the projector that he "won't do anything more than shoot a punkin and churn."

No plan of grouping the folk expressions can be altogether logical, but I have followed the laws of association in order to give the most convenient arrangement possible. I wish to acknowledge considerable indebtedness to my friend, Viola Fontaine Corley, of Mexia, Texas, for helping me to gather material here used.

SAYINGS IMPLYING DERISION

Every fellow to his own notion, as the old woman said when she kissed the cow.

I've seen wilder heifers than you milked in a gourd, ma'am.

Teach your grannie how to suck eggs!
Teach your grannie how to pick ducks!

Just as well go out and bay at the moon as ask that old skin-flint for money.

He might as well be singing psalms over a dead horse as trying to

make a doctor out of that boy of his (or attempt anything considered preposterous).
He might as well try to eat sugar (or soup) with a knitting needle.
I might as well look for a needle in a haystack.

That cooked his goose.

They'll live at the top of the pot for a while, I reckon (live high).

He thinks he's some punkins.

He'll shoot a punkin and churn; that's what he'll do.   (He'll "make a fizzle," "play Hob.")

He hasn't got sense enough to get in out of the rain.
He hasn't got the sense that God promised a louse.
He hasn't got as much sense as a last year's bird nest with the bottom punched out.

He found a mare's nest; that's what he found.
He found what the little boy shot at.   (Nothing.)

He made that yarn out of whole cloth.

He does not amount to a hill of beans.
He's a mighty small potato in my estimation.
He's mighty small potatoes and few in a hill.
He amounts to about as much as a notch on a stick and the stick thrown away.

That's a pretty kettle of fish!
That's a nice mess!

Not if the court knows itself, I won't.

Anything he says cuts mighty little ice.

She rules the roost.
She wears the breeches.

When he says "frog," she jumps.

He has about as much use for that as a hog has for Sunday.
He has about as much use for that as a hog has for seven horns.
He has about as much use for that as a wagon has for five wheels.
He has about as much use for that as a hog has for a side-saddle.

He couldn't sell ice water in hell.

He rattles around in his office like one pea in a pod.

He has the gall of a brass monkey.
He has gall enough to do anything.
He has brass enough to do it.
He has brass enough to make a boiler and sap enough to fill it.

His feathers fell when I told him that.

He sits around like a notch on a stick.

He swallowed that yarn—hook, line, and sinker.
He jumped on to that like a duck on a June bug.

He played the wild (or the wilds) when he did that.
He played the mischief.
He just about played whaley.

He does not know A from Adam's off ox; does not know B from bull's foot.
She does not know A from izzard.   (Compare: She knows it from A to izzard; i.e., thoroughly.)

He's so ugly that he has to slip up on a dipper to get a drink out of it.
He's so ugly that he has to slip up on a looking glass to get a look at himself.
He's so ugly that they have to put him down in a well before the sun will rise.
He's ugly enough to turn sweet milk to clabber.

She's so cross-eyed that when she cries the tears run down her back.

The old codger's as slow as molasses in January; also, as slow as Christmas.

Every time he opens his mouth he puts his foot in it.   (Expressive of awkwardness.)

SAYINGS EXPRESSIVE OF DECEIT OR DISHONESTY

There's a nigger in the woodpile.
You'd better look out; there may be a bug under the chip.
I smelled a rat right away.

Oh, butter wouldn't melt in his mouth now. He's in the middle of a bad fix, got the worst kind of cold feet, and wants me to help him out.

He's as polite as a basket of chips; sugar wouldn't melt in his mouth.
He comes around smilin' like a basket of chips.

He's got a grin on him like a Cheshire cat.

I would not believe him if he swore to it on a stack of Bibles as high as his head.
I would not believe him if he swore it till he turned black in the face.

He'd steal the nickels off a dead man's eyes.
He'd rob his grandmammy's grave.

You want to look mighty sharp before you have any dealings with that bird; he's liable to skin out and leave you with the bag to hold.

He may have made *a great miration* over the place, but it's my private opinion that he has something up his sleeve.

SAYINGS OF MISCELLANEOUS IMPORT

You must have sewed that with a red hot needle and a burning thread, but it will never be seen on a galloping horse and him in a trot.

It made a noise like pourin' peas on a dried cow-hide. (This might be a description of any kind of sound, even of music.)

She has neither chick nor child.

I gloried in her spunk.

I'll ride Shank's pony, *or* mare (walk).

He'll wake up dead some fine morning.

He has the old Adam in him (the devil).
He has the old Nick in him.

He's goin' around with a chip on his shoulder.

He's a regular Strap Buckler; i.e., drinks like a fish.

His plans were knocked into a cocked hat.
I'll knock him windin' and brick-stinin' if he fools with me.
He'll just about get knocked into the middle of next week.
That knocked him sky-westward and crooked eastward.

He's too lazy to scare the flies out of his mouth.
He's too lazy to shuck corn if you gave it to him.
He's too lazy to live.

He's too mean to die.

They didn't even leave me a smell of that cake, chicken, etc.   (To be taken literally.)

They didn't even give him the cork to smell.   (May be taken literally but often used to express a perfect job of fleecing.)

The house was seven ways for Sunday.
The house was every way for Christmas.
It looked as if lightning had struck the place.   (All three phrases are expressive of confusion.)
Cars were going in every direction and seven ways for Sunday.

You could have knocked me down with a feather, I was that surprised.

What did you do that fer?
Cat's fur to make kittens' breeches.

The tune the old cow died of.

The old cow crossed the road because she crossed the road.   (A way of saying that a reason is not a reason.)

He ran his head into a hornet's nest; *or*, stirred up a hornet's nest.

Then hell broke loose in Georgia.

Put that in your pipe and smoke it.

He told me that out of his own mouth.

She's one of the old blue hen's chickens; i.e., a "hell cat," a termagant.

They just literally limb-skinned and jay-hawked that tree.

She has on a brand splinterfire new dress.
She's flirting like a Spanish filly.
She's painted up like a wild Indian.

No monkey business wanted around here.

There are more ways to kill a dog than to choke him to death with butter.
There are more ways than one of breaking a dog from sucking eggs.

You could ride to mill on that knife without any blanket (it's so dull).
That knife would not cut hot butter in June.

He's in Dutch now (in bad).
He's in a regular jack-pot now.
He's up Salt Creek (in trouble).

He made his pile and now he's in clover.

That's no skin off my back.   (Nothing to me.)

Advice ran off him like water off a duck's back.
As well argue with a wooden Indian (or wooden man).

I killed him too dead to skin.   (The death is likely to be figurative, as in an argument.   To understand the figure it must be remembered that an animal that has been dead a long time is too putrified to skin.)

It's cold enough to freeze the horns off a billy goat.
It's cold enough to freeze the ears off a brass monkey.
Everything's frozen as stiff as stilliards.

It's so dark you can't see your hand before you.

His name is Dennis.   (He's "a gonner," doomed to go under.)
His name is Mud.

He could not hit the side of a house.

I don't know him from Adam's off ox.
I don't know him from the side of sole leather.

Not worth a tinker's dam.
I wouldn't give a tinker's dam for it.

That beats a hen a-scratchin'.
Don't that just beat a hen a-lopin'?

Everything's closed as tight as a drum.

Just hold your horses till I get through.   (Be patient.)
Keep your shirt on.
Don't kick till you are spurred.
Hold your potatoes.
You hold your potato till mine gets cold.

Keep your eye peeled (or skinned) for trouble.

He pulled his freight in a hurry.
He ran like the devil was after him.

He's steppin' eleben now (stepping high).
He's settin' purty.

Wait till we see how the land lies.   (Comprehend the whole situation.)
Wait till we see how the cat jumps.

The chickens will come home to roost.   (This means in a bad sense what "cast your bread upon the waters," etc., means in a good sense.)

A rich man for luck and a poor man for children.
Rich people have mean ways and poor people poor ways.

Them as has must lose, 'cause them as hasn't can't.

He's too big for his breeches.
He's got the swell head.
His hat's gettin' too small.

He'll get hanged as high as Haman.
That horse will throw him so high that the birds'll build nests in his ears before he hits the ground.

She gives me the hebe-jebes (also, the heaves).

The rain was a regular gully washer and fence-lifter (also, a gully washer and root-searcher).
It's raining bull frogs and heifer yearlings.
It's raining pitchforks.
It's raining cats and dogs.

I wouldn't marry him if he was the last man on God's green earth.
I wouldn't marry him if every hair in his head was strung with gold.

That galoot's not worth the powder and lead it would take to blow him up.
That guinea's not worth his salt (also, not worth his found).

They've got money (or anything else) galore.

She's sashayin' (or galavatin') all over the country.

Every man for himself and the devil take the hindmost.
Lord, take care of the poor and us rich devils will look out after ourselves.

I've a crow to pick with you.
I've a row to hoe with you.

He's a regular wheelhorse when it comes to doing work.
He's a stem-winder and go-getter.

You can't hear your ears in this place.
You couldn't hear yourself think.

That's a feather in his cap.

Miss Emma has set her cap for that young man.

That's a horse of another color.
That's a grey mare of a different color.
The shoe is on the other foot now.

She's all wool and a yard wide (a thoroughbred).

He sold out—lock, stock, and barrel.
He made a clean sweep of it while he was at it.

You hit the nail on the head that time.

He's playing second fiddle now.

He's still on the fence.

He's up to his neck in business.

The town's not much more than a grease spot in the middle of the road.
The town's just a wide place in the road.

He's a jack of all trades (and master of none).

Everything's lovely and the goose is hanging high.
All's well on (or along) the Potomac.

That was the last button on old Gabe's coat.
That was the straw that broke the camel's back.

I took my foot in my hand and walked.   (An expression of independence.)
Paddle your own canoe.

He spit on his hands and took a fresh start.

He's down to his last dollar now.
They're scraping the bottom of the flour barrel.
The wolf's at the door.

She wears her heart on her sleeve.

That's where the trail ends.   (That's all.)

That buck had a set of antlers on him that looked like a rocking chair.

When I told him that he had to fork up $500, he bellered like a bay
steer.

This pony paces like a rocking chair.

Work (run, do anything) like all forty.

Swear like a trooper.

Sweating like a nigger at election.

Not room enough to cuss a cat in.
Not room enough to turn around in.

His eyes bugged out (or bulged out) till you could have roped them with a grapevine.

A voice on him like the bulls of Bashan.

He cussed, fought, hollered, sang (etc.) from who laid the chunk.

Leaks like a riddle.

Out of the frying pan into the fire.
Between the devil and the deep blue sea.
Between two fires.

Got his dander up.

Layovers to catch meddlers.   (A curious answer made to inquisitive children.   What is the origin?)
Like the devil just down from the Klondike.

Looking like a drowned rat; like a wet chicken.

He looked as if his tongue was about ready to hang out; as if he'd seen a ghost; as if he'd been sent for and couldn't come.

We'll put the big pot in the little one; also, put the big pot in the little one and fry the skillet.   (Celebrate, have a regular *blow-out*— a word used long before the automobile was invented.)

SIMILES

As fit as a fiddle.

As bare as my hand; as bare as a bone.

As strong as an ox.

As full as a tick.

As sour as vinegar.

As flat as a flounder.

As crooked as a dog's hind leg; as crooked as a snake.   So crooked that he could not hide behind a corkscrew.

As thin as a rail.

As tall as a post.

As dry as powder (or, as a powder magazine).

As round as a ball.

As ugly as homemade sin; as ugly as a mud fence.

As rich as Croesus; as rich as Jay Gould; as rich as cream.

As dull as a froe.

As straight as a poker; as straight as a ramrod; as straight as an arrow.

As straight as a crow flies.   (Refers to direction.)

As white as a sheet; as pale as a ghost.

As sweet as sugar.

As nice as pie.

As snug as a bug in a rug.

As happy as a bedbug; as happy as if he had good sense; as happy as a bird; as happy as a June bug.

As pretty as a speckled pup under a new-painted buggy; as pretty as a speckled hen; as pretty as a picture.

As plump as a young pullet; as plump as a partridge.

As funny as a crutch.

As sharp as a gimlet; as sharp as a razor; as smart as a whip; as smart as a brier.

As crazy as a bedbug; as crazy as a bat; as crazy as a loon; as crazy as a *paisano* (road-runner or chaparral bird).

As hard as a brickbat; as hard as nails.

As deaf as an adder; as deaf as a post.

As weak as water; as weak as a kitten.

As sick as a dog.

As poor as a snake; as poor as a whippoorwill.   (Physical state.)
As poor as Job's turkey; as poor as a churchmouse; as poor as pig tracks.   (Economic condition.)

As plain as an old shoe.   (Character.)
As plain as the nose on your face.   (Logically speaking.)

As dark as a stack of black cats; as dark as Egypt; as dark as pitch; as dark as a dungeon.

As still as a mouse; as still as death.

As quick as a wink; as quick as a flash.
As fast as greased lightning.

As playful as a pup.
As skittish as a colt.

As mad as a wet hen; as mad as a hornet; as mad as hops.

As tight as Dick's hat band (which an old negro said was so tight that it "busted").

As smooth as a whistle.
As slick as a dime.
As slick as a button.   (Implying dishonesty.)

As bright as a new dollar; as bright as day.

As sure as shootin'; as sure as my name is ——————; as sure as a rock; as sure as you live; as sure as you're born.

As clear as mud (ironical); as clear as a bell; as clear as a whistle.

As dead as a door nail; as dead as Heck, or, as Heck's pup.

As hungry as a sow with seventeen sucking pigs; as hungry as a wolf.

As common as a yellow-mouthed suck-egg dog; as common as pig tracks; as common as dirt.

As bold as brass; as bold as a lion.

As high as Gilderoy's kite.

As tough as whip leather; as tough as bull hide.

As cold as ice; as cold as Flugians; as cold as kraut; as cold as thunder; as cold as the mischief.

As hot as blue blazes in hell; as hot as the mischief; hot enough to scorch a lizard on a fence rail; hot enough to scorch a lizard.

As thick as thieves (expression of intimacy); as thick as hops; as thick as my foot, as thick as hairs on a dog's back (expression of quantity).

As scarce as hen's teeth.

As wild as a buck; as wild as a deer; as wild as a *javelin* hog.

As big as all creation; as big as all outdoors; as big as a mule; as big as life; as big as a horse; as big as a barn door; as big as the side of a house; as big as a frog in a mill pond.
He has a heart in him as big as a skinned ox.

As black as the ace of spades; as black as my hat; as black as the back. (This last comparison may refer either to black soot in the back of the fireplace or to the back of the Bible.)

As green as grass; as green as a gourd.

As red as blood.

As yellow as a "punkin"; as yellow as saffron.

As grey as a rat.

As stubborn as a mule; as hard-headed as a mule.

As particular as an old maid.

As honest as the day is long.

As regular in his habits as a clock.

Eyes as big as saucers.

SAYINGS CONCERNING TIME

That happened when the old cow died.

As old as the hills.

I can do it in two shakes of a sheep's tail.
We'll have it done in three shakes of a dead sheep's tail.
I'll have it done before you can say "Jack Robinson" (before you can say "scat").

That will hold till hell freezes over; or, till hell freezes over and a little while on the ice.

Not till doomsday.

Since the year one.
Since Christ was a child.
Since Heck was a pup.
Since kingdom come.

What happened next?   Why, I went over the hill to hunt the turkeys then.

PROVERBS

Say nothing and saw wood.

You can't get blood out of a turnip.

Never cross the bridge till you get to it.

Don't count your chickens before they hatch.

Make hay while the sun shines.

Don't cry over spilt milk.

Feed a cold and (you will have to) starve a fever.

Belly full, heart easy.

You can lead a horse to water but you can't make him drink.

NICKNAMES

These seem to be characters out of school readers:
Meddlesome Mattie.
Stingy Peter.

Silly Billy.
Pretty Polly.

EXCLAMATIONS

I'll be horn-swoggled!

By the great horned-spoon!

The devil and Tom Walker!

Great Caesar's ghost!

I'll be switched!

Well, I just swanee!

Laws a-massy!

Oh, law!   (Presumably a corruption of Oh, Lawd!)

What in the old Scratch?

Shucks!

Fiddlesticks!

Hell and high water!

By Ned, by Jove, by jinks, by Jehoshaphat, by Henry, by granny, by gravy, by gum, by gracious, by jiggers, by gatlins, etc.

COLLECTIVES

The whole cavayard, outfit.   (From *caballada*, Spanish for a herd or bunch of horses; a term in common use all over the ranch country of the Southwest.)

The whole kit and bilin' of 'em.

The whole outfit.

The whole kaboodlum.

The whole kit and posse.

The whole shootin' match.

THE TOURNAMENT IN TEXAS

By J. Frank Dobie

In preparing this paper I am much indebted to Mrs. Robert P. Siddall, of Anderson, Texas, and to Mr. Branch Isbell, Odessa, Texas, each of whom has contributed an account of the tournament in Texas as practiced during the years following the Civil War. I myself had made some notes on the subject and had planned to write an account of the tournament as practiced in Live Oak County a quarter of a century past. Mrs. Siddall and Mr. Isbell agreed that it would be best to amalgamate all three accounts into one article.

Seventy-five years ago Sir Walter Scott was the most widely read writer in the South; some traveler, whose name I cannot now recall, went so far as to declare that Sir Walter Scott had made a large party in the South royalistic and that the ultimate result of a successful secession would be a southern monarchy! The Old South was *cavalier* in both the original and derived uses of the word: its gentlemen were horsemen. Familiar, then, as it was, through *Ivanhoe* and other romances, with the tournaments of feudal times, feudalistically as it was tending before the Civil War with its castes and its slaves, and proud and proficient as its men were in horsemanship, the Old South very naturally made of the tournament one of the most popular and manly of all sports as well as one of the most formal of all social practices.

As early as 1850, the tournament, in conjunction with the barbecue, was a gala occasion in such a representative Texas community as Montgomery, Montgomery County,[1] and it is likely that the tournament was "run" in this state at even an earlier date, the custom no doubt having been brought from older Southern states. "People came thirty and forty

---

[1] "Old Montgomery," by Anna Landrum Davis, Montgomery, Texas, in *The Texas History Teachers' Bulletin*, University of Texas, edited by W. P. Webb, Vol. XIII, No. 1, Dec. 8, 1925, p. 46.

miles" to take part in the Montgomery barbecues and tournaments.   After the Civil War the sport was resumed in Montgomery as in other places and was exceedingly popular all
over the South.

However elaborate the tournament might become, the first
step in preparation was usually very simple.   Some sporty
individual or group would generally announce that a tournament was to be held, and by the appointed time details of
it, the barbecue, and the ball would somehow have been attended to and the whole country would turn out.

The tournament course, or track, was 200 yards long in
a straight line.   There were three posts fifty yards apart,
the first one fifty yards from the starting point.   They were
set on the right-hand side of the track and stood about
ten feet high.   From the top of each post a horizontal beam
projected out three or four feet over the track.   From the
end of this beam a stiff wire dropped down about shoulder high
to a man on horseback.   An inch or so from its lower end
the wire was bent at a right angle so as to point towards
the termination of the track.   On this crook was hung an
iron or brass ring about two inches in diameter, wrapped
with cloth to make it more visible, sometimes white but
usually of mixed colors, such as red, white, and blue.   The
man running the tournament had a wooden pole, called a cue,
or lance, perhaps eight feet long, an inch or more in diameter
at the base and tapering to a fine point.   About three feet
from the base, or butt, of the cue was a leather guard to
protect the hand from being hit by the rings as they were
caught.   The object of the runners was to catch as many
rings as possible.   Each entrant was allowed to run three
times, and thus nine was the highest number of rings it was
possible to collect.   The course had to be ridden in a dead
run, a time limit being imposed that ruled out slow riding.
In some instances hurdles were placed near the posts in
order to make running more uneven and thus the piercing
of the rings more difficult.   The runner guided his horse
with his left hand and held the cue with his right, sometimes
supporting the base of it along his arm or with the shoulder.
There were various ways of holding the cue, some preferring
one kind of grasp and some another.

The entrants were called "knights," and in their costumes

represented, according to their ideas and means, the dress
of King Arthur's court. Bright colored jackets, blouses and
sashes (in Southwest Texas, Mexican sashes), tightly fitting
trousers, and high-heeled boots with quilted tops were all in
style. Anybody who had a way to ride and who could ride
was privileged to enter "the lists," but each knight was
charged a small fee to help defray the expenses of the occasion.
The knights generally dubbed themselves with names expressive of the locality from which they hailed, as, "Knight of
Shanghai Springs," "Knight of Dry Branch," "Knight of the
Bragg Wright Thicket."

Before beginning the run for tournament rings, the knights
all mounted and paraded. In the middle eastern section of
Texas, says Mrs. Siddall, "they wheeled and marched in fours.
The horses were groomed until their bodies and hoofs glis-
tened, and sometimes their manes were braided with gay ribbons. The saddles were elaborately embossed and stamped,
the blankets under them brightly colored."

After the order in which the knights were to run had been
determined, each ran one time. Then in the same order
the knights ran a second and a third time. This method made
for much more suspense than having a knight make all three
runs in immediate succession; furthermore, it allowed the
horses to get their wind between courses. At the conclusion
of the tournament, first, second, and third winners were announced. The first prize was a crown ("of some glittering
stuff") and the second and third prizes were wreaths. "In
later days," to quote Mrs. Siddall again, "the prizes were
jewelry, and the knights' costumes were of velvet and silk,
lace-trimmed, with knee trousers and buckled shoes."

As the prizes were announced, the successful knights rode
or stepped forth to receive them. Then with great formality
each in turn presented his guerdon to the lady of his choice,
craving her "gracious acceptance." Mr. Branch Isbell ran
the tournament in Alabama before coming to Southwest Texas,
and, in that state, he says, "I was once fortunate enough to
win a wreath. I gave it to a lady some years my senior with
the original lines quoted below, which I had in anticipation
burned the midnight oil composing:

Fair lady, take this wreath,
   And though its flowers may fade upon thy marble brow,
The day on which I gave it thee
   Shall ever be as fresh within my memory as now.

I can't say how the lady felt at that moment, but I opined that the world was at my feet and that my greatest earthly ambition had been attained."

Before the "Sap" Railroad (the San Antonio & Aransas Pass) was built to Corpus Christi and Alice, Lagarto (the words means alligator) was the best town in Live Oak County, furnishing ranch supplies for a large section of country and outfitting cowboys for many a herd of horses and cattle headed up the old Chisholm Trail. When the time is seasonable, gentle reader, I expect to write a Lamb-like essay on "Lagarto Five-and-Thirty Years Ago," for in barefooted boyhood I walked or galloped my horse through the sand weekly for the mail, watched Bud Goodwin, Frank Beall, and his brothers who owned the store follow its shadow with their dollar pitching, and dreamed of the time when I might be wealthy enough to buy all the striped stick candy in it. In 1885—before my birth—Lagarto had a tournament, and I quote the following report of it from the Corpus Christi *Caller* of September 27, 1885 (reprinted in the issue of September 27, 1925) :

"The first anniversary of the Lagarto College was celebrated in grand style on Saturday, September 26, 1885, with tournament, barbecue, vocal and instrumental music, speeches, recitations, etc. At least a thousand persons were in attendance, the people coming from far and near in buggies, ambulances, and other kinds of vehicles, as well as on horseback. At 10 o'clock the young men who were to run in the tournament marched away from the Faupel Hotel, mounted on their chargers, towards the grounds, with R. J. Dobie [my father to be] at the head of the procession as master of ceremonies. The knights were followed by Professor Faupel and his brass band, some seventeen musicians, in addition to a band from Beeville on foot, making the woods [the "woods" around Lagarto consist of mesquite bushes and prickly pear] ring with their lively airs. The boys in their costumes, carrying flags and lances, reminded one of a lot of cavalry. Two prizes, both gold medals, were given to the knights taking the greatest number of rings. Names of the knights running in the contest: P. E. McNeill, W. E. McNeill, V. G. Miller, James Little, Charles Lawrence, Leslie McNeill, Ernest Miller, John Beall, J. H. Newberry, Ed Dubose, Albert Maley, and R. Dugat.

"At twelve o'clock the large assemblage had a real feast of barbecued meat. Theodore Lawrence and John Priour were on hand with a wagon load of ice, lemons, soda water, etc., from Corpus Christi. Among the attendants were three county judges, . . . two sheriffs, . . . and two newspaper reporters, W. D. Owens of the San Antonio *Express* and E. T. Merriman of the Corpus Christi *Caller.*

"At 8 P. M. the college building was packed to its utmost capacity, . . . the entertainment opening with calisthenic exercises performed by twenty pupils, with Miss Ella Newberry playing at the piano. This was followed by young ladies' singing and addresses by S. G. Miller, president of the college, by Dr. Bourlan of Georgia, and by Professor Faupel, instructor of music. . . . Then followed declamations by a number of the young men, some of them speaking in Spanish. A speech on education was delivered by Judge Moses, followed by an able address from Professor W. Y. Taylor, principal of the college. In the list of teachers the following names appear: P. G. Morris, Luis Puebla, and Miss Ella Byler [who two years later became Mrs. R. J. Dobie]."

Thus in days only forty years past did the tournament share in "college honors." Today it is as forgotten as the old town of Lagarto—the grounds of its "college" and its "hotel" inhabited by the lizard that pants upon the barren sands or hides under the shade of mesquite bushes. But before the tournament became totally extinct, it was for a brief while towards the opening of the present century revived in a very different form from the older tournament. Of this revival I have many and joyous memories, and it seems proper to record some of them here.

The setting is Live Oak County. As in former years the tournament was usually held in connection with a barbecue or basket picnic. A barbecue required the coöperation of the substantial citizens of the country, for they furnished the beef to barbecue. A ranchman might contribute a calf, yearling, or steer; or he might contribute money to help buy beef. The committee sponsoring the barbecue arranged for beef, bread, and pickles; the "women folks" usually brought salads, cakes, and pies. At a basket picnic all eatables were brought by families of the country, but there was always a crowd of young men and politicians who depended on campground invitations to get something to eat. Such was the custom of the country and invitations were plentiful and hearty. A big barbecue always had a Mexican "band," two or three Mexicans with accordion, violin, and guitar. All day long they played "La Paloma," "La Golondrina," "El Abandonado," and other favorites, mostly waltzes. It was haunting music, and the strains of it came to my ears out of the *huajillo* brush all the way home, lingered through a night of dreams, and did not entirely die away for several days.

After dinner the tournament would begin. It had lost all flavor of the days when knighthood was in flower. Cowboys and farmer boys who wanted to be cowboys were the participants, some of them in the habiliments of a brush-hand— leather leggins and ducking jacket—but most of them in their "Sunday clothes," which permitted boots but more regularly required patent leather shoes. The entrants paid two or three dollars apiece to run and the prizes were purchased with "the pot." The worth of the prizes would thus depend upon the number of entrants. At one big barbecue I remember a fine P. Bauer saddle (Paul Bauer and Tom Sonley, both of Beeville, being the best known saddle makers in the country). Leather leggins, hand-forged bridle-bits, fancy hackamores (halters), silver plated "gal's leg" spurs (so called because the shank of the spur represented the lower part of a "gal's leg"), bright colored manila ropes: such things were the prizes. There was frequently a good deal of betting among both spectators and participants. Many of the church people looked upon the tournament runners as children of the devil. I was hardly old enough to run against the mature or rapidly maturing contestants, but I knew that if I did enter the lists, my strict parents—the father who fifteen years before had been master of tournament ceremonies at Lagarto and the mother who at another time had been crowned as "Queen of Love and Beauty"—would interfere.

Nevertheless, my oldest brother and I had a tournament

course at home on our ranch, and I imagine that my father helped us to make it. There was another tournament course on the Hinnant Ranch, which cornered against ours, but I do not recall that there were any other private courses in the country around us. Running the tournament is the best sport I have ever taken part in. Catching the rings called for real skill—for steady nerves, keen eyesight, and adroit horsemanship; it called also for a good horse. A rough, high-jumping horse was no good here, however good he might be in hurdling over prickly pear. A smooth-running pony of polo size was most desirable. I had a bay, white-faced, and stocking-footed horse called Buck that, to my young mind, was the best tournament horse in Live Oak County. At this minute I would give twenty-five dollars to be on old Buck with cue in hand, going at full speed down the tournament track. Our track was in rather sandy soil, and we ran on it so much and the drouth was so persistent that after a while the sand became too heavy for a horse to run in. By the time I was sent off to a high school (1904) the tournament craze was a thing of the past. Perhaps it will come back some day. I recommend it to an age looking for something fresh and full of motion.

Some months ago Mr. Philip C. Tucker of Davenport, Florida, presented the Texas Folk-Lore Society, of which he is an enthusiastic member, with a copy of *Tallahassee of Yesterday*, by Sallie E. Blake, Tallahassee, Florida, 1924. The book prints a long extract from a newspaper, *The Floridian*, of January, 1870, describing in orthodox Southern floweriness of the day, a tournament that had just been held near Tallahassee. The extract is quoted here as giving a very detailed picture of the custom. I doubt if the tournament in Texas was ever quite so softly sentimental as the *Floridian* reports it to have been "in Leon County."

The Tournament is universally recognized, we believe, as a Southern institution, and one that has ever enlisted the sympathies of the young men of this section. Its feats of daring chivalry are particularly attractive to those of Huguenot descent, who, unlike the descendants of the straight-laced Puritans, find a vast fund of enjoyment in its exciting contests. The ladies, too, from time immemorial, have endorsed the feats of the tourney by their presence and approving words, and beneath their sweet glances it cannot be wondered at that such contests have been encouraged to the utmost by the rising men of the South.

Animated by such sentiments as swelled the bosoms of such chivalric knights as Richard Coeur de Lion, and wishing to revive a time honored custom which extensively prevailed in the South in ante-bellum times, but which, for many reasons, has been allowed to languish of late, the young men of Leon County formed an organization, which was to culminate in a grand contest of skill and lance in the presence of the assembled daughters of Leon, for such prizes as are usually awarded on those occasions.

The old field in the rear of Judge Dannely's residence, about a mile and a half to the northward of the city, where in the good old days of yore many a contest between brave and skillful knights had taken place, was selected for the present Tournament, and last Friday was agreed upon as the day which should witness the ceremony. The day dawned lovely. Old Sol shone brightly forth in a clear and placid sky, and at the hour of ten o'clock a.m., vehicles of every conceivable description, filled with visions of loveliness and beauty, thronged the road leading to the grounds, while pedestrians were almost too numerous to be counted, from the fact that every conveyance which could be had for either love or money was already engaged. By eleven o'clock the grounds were literally covered with spectators eager to witness the feats of skill and arm by the Knights of Leon and their colleagues, who were now rapidly approaching the scene of action. Upon their arrival the Knights were drawn up in line, in front of the assembled multitude, when Mr. George F. Raney, the orator of the day, delivered an appropriate oration in which he referred to the past days of chivalry; reminding the Knights of the memories clustering around their order, and pointing to the fair ladies there assembled to witness and reward with approving smiles their deeds of activity and valor. The Knights soon filed down the line under the command of Captain R. B. Burroughs, field marshal, and were drawn up at the starting point in the following order:

JEFFERSON COUNTY

Mr. V. W. Partridge, Knight of Ravenswood.
Mr. W. Budd, Osceola, the bare-back rider.
Mr. T. W. Tucker, Roland of Avenel.
Mr. George Footman, Knight of the Golden Fleece.
Dr. B. Simkins, Knight of the Border.
Mr. R. B. Whitfield, Knight of Clermont.

GADSDEN COUNTY

Mr. G. A. Colson, Knight of Gadsden.

LEON COUNTY

Mr. W. Perkins, Malcolm Grahame.
Mr. George Houston, Knight of Malta.
Mr. John Hopkins, Knight of Greenwood.
Mr. George R. Ward, James Fitz-James.
Mr. H. C. Damon, Knight of Crescent.
Mr. W. Felkel, Knight of La Grange.
Dr. Julius Carn, Knight of the Red Cross.
Mr. Thomas Archer, Knight of the Golden Horse Shoe.
Mr. ——————, The Unknown Knight.

Three arches, with a ring suspended from each, had been erected at intervals of about fifty yards. The starting point was about ninety yards distant from the first arch, and fifteen seconds were allowed each Knight to make the whole distance. Col. George W. Scott, Capt. L. E. Johnson, and Mr. A. Hopkins acted as judges, and Mr. T. P. Myers and A. L. Woodward, Jr., as heralds. The costumes of the Knights were neat and exceedingly appropriate, and mounted upon symmetrical steeds they promised to give fine sport to the company then and there assembled.

Anxious was the gaze of every one, especially the ladies, as the bugle sounded the charge and the Knight of Ravenswood commenced the exercises of the day, as with well poised lance he sped forward like the wind and with triumph bore off the first ring. He was followed by Osceola, the bare-back rider, who met with similar success. The other Knights soon completed their first run, none taking more than one ring excepting the Knight of Malta, who carried off two rings successfully.

The second run was perhaps more successful than the first, although a want of practice was plainly perceptible on the part of many of the Knights, some of whom were on the ground for the first time. In this contest two rings were taken off by the Knights of the Golden Horse Shoe and Greenwood, and by James Fitz-James, and eager must have been the expectations of the fair damsels for whom these chivalric Knights so gallantly rode.

After an intermission of a few minutes to allow both horses and men to recuperate, the third run commenced, and as the Knight of Malta rode through, carrying off the whole number of rings, making six in the three runs, he was greeted with loud shouts of applause, for it seemed evident that he would win the crown. And so the sequel proved, for no other Knight bore off more than five rings altogether. James Fitz-James caught five rings and thus gained the privilege of selecting the First Maid of Honor. The other honors fell upon the Knights of Greenwood and the Golden Horse Shoe. The tilt being completed, every one was of course anxious to know whom the Knight of Malta would designate as the Queen of Love and Beauty. With such an array of beauty and loveliness as was exhibited upon the ground, a choice would seem to have been attended with no little embarrassment, but the successful Knight doubtless had a fair one in view when he entered the lists, for he had no hesitation in making his choice.

The Knights were soon drawn up in front of the vehicle occupied by Miss Bettie Douglass, when the Knight of Malta advanced bearing upon the point of his lance an artistically wrought crown, with which, after an appropriate speech by the orator of the day, he decorated her brow, saying: "With this chaplet I crown thee Queen of Love and Beauty." The compliment was received with that becoming modesty with which the daughters of Leon are pre-eminently distinguished. The Queen was soon joined by Misses H. Screven, N. Gamble, and M. Ward, who were selected as her Maids of Honor.

The carriage with its precious freight, surrounded and guarded by all the Knights, then moved off in the direction of the city, amid the enthusiastic plaudits of the crowd, many of whom joined in the procession and swelled the Royal train. Arrived in town, the lovely Queen and her elegant Maids of Honor were all safely escorted by the gallant Knights to their respective places of abode, and all then dispersed to prepare for the Grand Fancy Ball which was to come off in the evening.

The Assembly very kindly permitted their hall to be used for the ball-room, and the desks, railing and carpet were removed and everything was arranged for the dance. At an early hour in the evening, the Knights and invited friends began to assemble, and the hall was soon crowded with fair women and brave men. Seldom, if ever, have we seen such a magnificent display of beauty and fashion. The Queen and her Maids of Honor were elegantly attired and promenaded the hall with graceful dignity, being the observed of all observers. The Knights appeared in the costumes worn in the Tournament, while a great portion of the ladies were in costume, admired by all who surrounded them.

Among the most prominent characters represented was La Fille du Regiment, personated by Mrs. L. E. Johnson. Her glistening epaulettes, miniature drum, and canteen enlisted the attention of all present. "Night," robed as black as Erebus, wearing a mantle profusely studded with golden stars, was represented by Miss Archer, and was universally admired. Miss Lewis, as Cupid, the God of Love, bearing the fatal bow and a quiver well stocked with envenomed darts, excited a great amount of attention, her little silver shaft being aimed promiscuously among the gay bachelors present, and kept, we doubt not, by many of her victims as welcome souvenirs of the past. Miss Mary Perkins, as the Highland Lassie, won warm encomiums for the correct and faultless style of costume she had selected for the occasion. Perhaps the most original and attractive costume was that worn by Miss Argyle, who appeared as a representative of the press, her dress being made entirely of newspapers, while upon a narrow scarf she wore most gracefully was printed conspicuously, "The Floridian." We doff our best hat to our lady friend in honor of the delicate compliment conveyed and can assure her that it was fully appreciated by ourselves.

The Senate Chamber was laid out as a supper room, where a number of tables groaned beneath a liberal and elegant display of the choicest and richest viands, and as the band pealed forth a stately march the gay assemblage filed gracefully in to the festive board, where in place of dry and uninteresting debates, loud and joyous laughter, capital jokes, toasts and sentiments became the order of the evening. If any one present failed to be in a capital good humor it was certainly his own fault. After supper was dispatched, the dancing was resumed in the hall, and continued until a late hour, leaving every one perfectly satisfied with the Tournament and its attendant enjoyments, and hoping to witness an annual repetition of the same.

EPISODES AT RANCH COMMUNITY DANCES IN TEXAS FIFTY-FIVE YEARS AGO[1]

By Branch Isbell

As I grew up in Sumter County, Alabama, I participated in various dancing parties before emigrating to Texas to become a cowboy. When I reached Nueces County, Texas, in company with Mr. Frank Byler, who had "been east" with horses to sell and who had promised me a job if I would return with him, I was just nineteen years of age. Mr. Byler lived at "The Motts," or Nuecestown, fourteen miles up the Nueces River from Corpus Christi. I arrived in January, 1871, and soon became acquainted with everyone in the little village. I learned that all over Southwest Texas the people outside of the few larger towns lived in similar villages or "settlements" for mutual protection against raiding parties of Mexicans or Indians.

At that time dancing was the most common amusement, and before and after each big cow-hunt it was the custom for some family to give a dance to speed the parting cowboys or to welcome their return. The music employed often consisted of a single fiddle or accordion, but sometimes two or three other stringed or wind instruments were added. Most of the dancers danced only old Virginia reels or cotillions, but some of each sex were experts in jigs and the so-called "round dances," polkas, waltzes, schottisches, and the like.

Sometimes very amusing and near tragic episodes were enacted at these gatherings. In 1872, just before starting on a cow-hunt, I got a companion to trim my hair, which had grown so long that I was afraid it might hang me up to a mesquite limb and cause me to share the fate of Absalom. My companion proved his tonsorial capacity by making my head look like a cross between an armadillo and a porcupine.

---

[1]For further information on the subject concerning which Mr. Isbell tells such delightful anecdotes, the reader is referred to "The Cowboy Dance," by John R. Craddock in *Publications* Number II (1923) of the Texas Folk-Lore Society and to "The Cowboy Dance of the Northwest," by Roy S. Scott in *Publications* Number IV (1925). See a brief sketch of Mr. Isbell in "Contributors" towards the end of this volume.—Editor.

That night we attended a dance, and as soon as we arrived, our host, noting my appearance, said to me: "Come, I want you to meet my daughter. That head will be a curiosity to her." Sure enough, when I was presented to the young lady with all the formality of the times, she seemed to view me not only with curiosity but with alarm.

I sauntered on around the room and became "the observed of all observers." After a while I returned to the girl and asked her if she would dance the next cotillion with me.

"No," she replied, "not looking as you do."

Thinking to retaliate with a cute answer, I said: "Thank you. I'll seek another partner, and please remember that there are as good fish in the sea as were ever caught out of it."

"Yes, sir, I'm familiar with that old saw," she fired back at me, "but unfortunately for you those wise fish have quit biting at toads."

I slunk out of the house and sat on the woodpile in the dark, morosely reflecting upon the futility of talking back at the feminine gender.

At a later dance a large wash-pot of coffee, surrounded with ample tin cups, was kept boiling under a live oak tree in the yard, so that the guests might refresh themselves whenever they desired to do so. While the cowboys and their partners danced inside the house, some tree lizards also engaged in dancing among the branches of that live oak tree.

Along toward morning a lady asked me to get her a cup of coffee. The supply being almost exhausted, I had to scrape the bottom of the pot to get it. Now, as it turned out, an awkward tree dancer had fallen into the pot and, all unaware of its presence, I scooped up the corpse with the liquid. Imagine the situation when the lady, after drinking the coffee, discovered that boiled lizard in the bottom of her cup. She almost fainted and she vomited copiously, while I, in the presence and hearing of the congregated dancers, condemned the lizard tribe to Hades in language that was not altogether Scriptural.

On another occasion a self important and windy young fellow was dancing a cotillion with his spurs jingling and his six-shooter belted around him. Ere long another of the same ilk and accoutrements took the place of a friend in the set.

Presently the two "careless looking" fellows jolted each other
and then each, appearing to be mortally offended, went for
his gun.   Two or three *compadres* (companions) caught each
of the belligerents and forced them outside into the moonlight.
At this juncture, an old-timer noted for nerve and determina-
tion drew *his* weapon and ordered the blood-hunters released.
His orders were obeyed.   Then he said: "Now shoot or leave
and whatever you are going to do, do it *pronto*."[2]

The "bad" young *hombres* vanished into the shadows in
opposite directions and the dance went merrily on.

Well, those old dances were long since "broken up," and
the dancers, most of them, have danced away after that
"Caller" whose last "call" we all must follow.   But before I
hear that last "call" I want to try my hand at—or, rather,
shake my feet in—an old time reel or cotillion or both, for, in
spite of my seventy-five years, they "linger in my memory like
a pleasant dream."

---

[2]"The herd we drove was half and half grown cows and steers, and
that season (1871) it was customary to kill young calves found on the
bed-ground.   I had a pistol and it was my duty to murder the innocents
each morning while their pitiful mothers were ruthlessly driven on.   It
looked hard, but circumstances demanded the sacrifice, and being the
executioner so disgusted me with six-shooters that I have never owned—
much less used—one from that time to this.   It is likely, too, that not
being a gun-man during the following five or six years kept me from
becoming involved in several shooting tragedies that I saw enacted.
Unpreparedness has kept me peacefully inclined."—Quoted from "Days
That Were Full of Thrills," by Branch Isbell, in *The Trail Drivers of
Texas*, Vol. II, edited by J. Marvin Hunter and published by George W.
Saunders, Union Stock Yards, San Antonio, Texas, 1923, pages 18–30.
Volumes I and II of *The Trail Drivers of Texas* have recently been re-
printed in one binding by Lamar and Barton, Dallas.—Editor.

PIONEER CHRISTMAS CUSTOMS OF TARRANT COUNTY

BY MARY DAGGETT LAKE

The early Christmas celebration in Tarrant County, as recalled by pioneer settlers, was very different from the celebration of today. The Christmas tree was hardly known, for
in those days the exchange of gifts was unheard of. However,
the children hung up their stockings, and Santa Claus brought
them nuts and apples. Fireworks are significant of the Fourth
of July in the North, but from the earliest time they have
added to the gaiety of the Christmas season in the South,
though the fireworks that lighted up the old-time Christmas
were rather crude. Holes were bored in logs, and powder
was poured into them. Then with the aid of pocket knives and
a piece of punk, the charge was touched off. Some of the boys
"managed" for their mother's carpet rags, which they rolled
into balls, soaked in oil, lighted, and tossed into the air.

Every Christmas in that day was more or less a "community Christmas." A few weeks ahead, a number of men would
make wagon trips to Marshall or Houston for supplies. Coffee,
sugar, and other commodities that are necessities with us
today, were rare luxuries to those early settlers. These
freighting trips bespoke a good Christmas, if the men returned
in time, for the occasion much more than Thanksgiving was
celebrated with food and drink.

Hunting and fishing made contribution to the season in
food and sport. Prairie chickens, deer, antelopes, buffaloes,
rabbits, squirrels, and quail were all plentiful. Wild turkey
roosts were to be found in many parts of the county, but
certain places along Marine and Sycamore creeks were favorite haunts with the birds. The holiday turkey shoot was a
real occasion. The men would slip up on the turkeys in the
darkness and either skylight them and shoot them or else
keep still and wait for breaking day to outline the target better.
More than once, however, hunters in the darkness met other
hunters and, mistaking them for game, shot them down.
Around Christmas time the fur is freshest and thickest on
animals, and that was a favorite season for hunting the

'possum and the coon with dogs. The skins were either used or sold.

The occasional discovery of a bee tree added to the larder. Those who could afford other sweets had great pies and cakes. Fruits were scarce, but nuts were more common. Everybody had coffee and eggnog. For very many people Christmas simply would not have been Christmas without a flowing bowl of eggnog along with clove scented apple dumplings and rich mince pies.

Music and the dance played an important part in the early Christmas celebration. Musical instruments were not easily to be had, but a French harp or a common fiddle then went as far as an orchestra goes now. The White Settlement boasted the first pianos in the country, and the homes that possessed these pianos were centers of social life and the scenes of many Christmas festivities. Dr. M. L. Woods and family came to Tarrant County during the time of the old fort, in 1853, bringing with them their piano, one of the earliest makes of the grand. It is of mahogany and rosewood, and has a keyboard much smaller than the ordinary piano. However, the tonal qualities are not surpassed by the pianos of today. This piano is in a splendid state of preservation, and is the property of Dr. Woods' descendants living in Fort Worth. In 1856, Mr. and Mrs. John A. Mitchell located in Tarrant County, and Mrs. Mitchell brought her piano from Memphis, Tennessee, to Shreveport, Louisiana, by water and then to Fort Worth by ox wagon. This piano was en route from Shreveport to Fort Worth three months. Mrs. Mitchell was a gifted pianist and was also Tarrant County's first music teacher.

It will never be known just how much the early settlers of Texas owed to the stirring notes of the fiddle. Certain it is that every home, cross-roads store, and community had its fiddler, and so much a part of the man was his fiddle that they were scarcely ever seen apart. A story is told on Jack M. Durrett, as great a lover of music as ever drew a bow—and a sweet one too he could draw. His house caught fire while he was singing and playing "The Arkansas Traveler." Amid all the excitement incident upon such an emergency, "Uncle Jack" went right on with his fiddling. When told of the fire, in place of the line, "Why don't you play the rest of that tune?" he improvised, "Boys, please go put it out," and continued with his piece. When asked afterwards why he didn't stop and help put the fire out, he replied, "Damn it, I was in a place where I couldn't stop."

Parties of various kinds were indulged in at Christmas. Card games were very popular, euchre and poker being the games most played. Dominoes, candy pulls, corn poppings, play-parties, and dancing furnished additional amusement. Most people in Tarrant County danced for diversion, especially at the holiday season, but some did not. Where there was strong religious conviction, sentiment was against dancing.

The dance was the one place where the fiddler was indispensable. Dancers were often kept all night and sometimes far into the morning with "Swing your partner," "Forward and back," and numerous other "calls" which accompanied the old time square dance. Those were the days of the "caller," who was frequently the fiddler as well. He was easily the most popular man in the country. Age was no barrier to the old time square dance. Babies and great-grandparents alike enjoyed the fun. To such tunes as "Pop Goes the Weasel," "Billy in the Low Ground," "Money Musk," "Sally Gooden," and "The Campbells are Coming," the dancers tripped the night away. Morning came, and slowly, by two's and in bunches, the crowd rode away across the prairie toward home.

Nothing delights the old-timer more than to tell of "the good old days" when "dancin' was dancin', and not wrastlin'." Let us roll back the curtain of life fifty or seventy years and look in on a dance. Certainly we would see "Uncle Buck" Adams, his brother Frank, Tom Moody, Jess Ferguson, L. Taylor, "Tede" Field, John Lane, "Uncle Jack" Durrett, and others of the old time "callers." One among them, the late E. M. (Bud) Daggett, veteran cattleman of Fort Worth, was a famous "caller" of that early day. He has painted a word picture of the old time dance.

"Fifty years and more ago, dances in Tarrant County were things of beauty. The steps demanded grace; the ladies and gents bowed without hunching their shoulders; the lady bent her head and courtesied to the floor, while the gent put his right hand over his heart, drew back one foot, and bowed

gracefully. Then there were steps. Why, I've seen a gent
go that high in the air (illustrated by holding his hand three
feet off the floor), and come down as light as a feather. No
noise at all. Not even his spurs jingled. Put these modern
dancers through the same paces and they'd make more noise
than a herd of stampeded cattle. I don't believe the young
folks who dance these new-fangled dances would know what
to do if I started calling figures. Not that they don't know
how to dance; I'm not saying that. All I know about them
is just what I have seen, but I will say that I don't like this
grapevine twisting.

"Every now and then we old folks have a little party
and dance some of the old time steps, and I can't help comparing them. What do you suppose one of these modern couples
would do if I should step out into the middle of the floor
and say, 'First lady and gent forward and back again; four
hands 'round, and first gent swing the lady on his right; forward and back again; honor your partners; balance and swing,
and promenade outside the ring'? Huh?" Daggett stopped
short and waited for an answer. The young man addressed
kicked at a bale of hay on a division platform at the stockyards,
and looked hopefully down the runway for another herd of
steers to give him inspiration. "I'll tell you," answered Daggett. "They'd 'hesitate'." Then he chuckled appreciatively
at his own little joke.

Dancing in those days differed in kind and degree as it
does today. There was the conventional dance with its ease
and grace. Then there was the cowboy dance, which was of
a different kind. The increase of the cattle industry in this
county brought the cowboys, and with their coming conven-
tionalities were more or less laid aside. Their favorite square
dance was characterized as "a cross-timber hoe down." They
disdained to swap their boots for dancing shoes. Pistols,
spurs, and chaps were not obstacles. Good natured horse-play
was the rule rather than the exception. Occasionally the fire
in a fair damsel's eyes would kindle the spirit of warfare in
the hearts of rival cowpunchers, and trouble would be the
result. These battles were "go-as-you-please" affairs, and the
epitaph of more than one gay Lothario of the plains was, "He
died with his boots on because the other fellow drew first."

Apart and far removed from the innocent joy and fun of the refined, were the revelries of the "punchers" held in various places along the "beef trail" of South and West Texas. Many pioneers will recall Pecan Grove, just northeast of Fort Worth, where cowpunchers of the roughest type gathered. Frequently they "shot up the shack" just for the fun of the thing, and rendered the night hideous.

Christmas came to the slave quarters as well as to the "big house." In that day every home had a large open rock fireplace, for stoves were not available. The negroes were promised a holiday lasting as long as the Yule log that they might bring in would burn. They had great fun in vying with each other as to who could bring in the largest log. Frequently it would require the efforts of several to bring in one. The "quarters" were always eagerly astir on Christmas morning, for it was the custom that the master would remember each negro in some fashion. The shouts of "Chrismus Gif', Marse John," "Chrismus Gif', Marse Charles," "Chrismus Gif', Miss Julie," have rung down through the years, and we recall a day that is gone.

SUPERSTITIONS OF BEXAR COUNTY

By E. R. Bogusch

Most of the superstitions here recorded have been gathered among the German farmers of Bexar County. Some of the beliefs have descended directly from the German colonists who settled there generations ago; others have been formed or modified by contact with negroes and Mexicans; many are the common property of folk all over America; many, also, belong to universal folk-lore.

Superstition yet has a living part in the lives of many German farmers of Bexar County. From childhood they have heard certain sayings so often that they accept them without question and repeat them without comment. The weather, as everywhere else, is a fertile topic for conversation, and some farmer in a group around the country post office will naturally remark: "Well, the pigs have been carrying straw all morning; so I guess we'll get something in the way of weather right soon." Another may yawn and remark: "I saw the pigeons flying high yesterday and that's a sure sign of rain."

So firm is the belief in some of these signs that certain men will swear that they have never known them to fail. On the other hand, many of the superstitions are frankly acknowledged as such. For instance, the cat may be asleep on the doorstep with its tail curled around its feet. "Go and see who is coming," the mother will say to one of the children, then turn and smilingly explain to the stranger, "It is just an old saying among ourselves that company will come from the direction towards which the cat's tail points."

In arranging the superstitions I have been unable to prevent some overlapping, for many beliefs contain more than one element. The weather signs are probably, as a class, more generally familiar than any other. A number of them have already been recorded in "Weather Wisdom of the Texas-Mexican Border," by J. Frank Dobie in *Publications* of the Texas Folk-Lore Society, Number II. My only reason for repeating them is to get in the aggregate the beliefs, or sayings, of one particular group of people.

WEATHER SIGNS

If the chickens stand in the rain, the rain will continue; but if they seek shelter, the rain will stop.

When a hen suns herself, rain or cold weather is coming soon.

If the rooster crows before nine o'clock, a norther is coming.

If the rooster crows after nine o'clock, the day will be foggy.

If the roosters crow after dark, rain will come.

Restlessness of geese indicates a storm.

If the ducks fly early in the fall, there will be a long, cold winter ahead.

When pigeons fly high and circle about, a strong wind is coming.

When the sea birds fly high, there will be a flood.

When the wasps fly into the house, rain is coming.

When flies enter the house, rain is coming.

If snails crawl up the side of a house, rain is coming.

When wolves howl, the weather will change.

If the pigs are busy all day carrying straw for a bed, a storm is coming.

If a pig has a straw in its mouth, rain is coming soon.

If the pigs run around in the pen, the weather will change.

If the cattle run about with their tails up, a storm is coming.

If the horses and mules snort and jump about, a norther is due.

When the leaves of the peach or mesquite tree become rusty, rain is not far away.

If a dry spring begins flowing again during a drought, rain will follow.

If a hole is punched in a can of rain water and the water drained out, there will be no more rain for a year.

If smoke falls after rising from the chimney, rain will come soon.

If the soot on the bottom of the coffee pot burns, it is going to rain.

If a person's stocking comes down, it is a sign of rain.

Where lightning strikes there is gold in the ground.

Lightning never strikes twice in the same place.

If the sky is cloudy in the morning, there will be no more rain that day.

If the sky clears at sunset, more rain will come the next day.

When the sun sends its rays through a dark bank of clouds, rain will come within twenty-four hours.

When the sun sends its rays through a dark bank of clouds, it is drawing water.

If the sky in the north looks black, there will be a blue norther.

If the storm passes away quietly, there will be more rain.

When there is much thunder and lightning, the weather will clear soon.

If the sun shines while rain is falling, the devil is beating his wife.

A long summer is followed by a very cold winter.

The kind of weather prevailing during the week of the twenty-first of September determines the severity of the winter.

Clearness of the sky on Good Friday forecasts a prosperous year.

If there is heavy thunder in September, there will be a good fruit crop the next year.

Seeds planted in the light of the moon will grow well above the ground, but will form few roots.

If the waning moon has both horns up, the month will be dry; but if the moon is tilted, the water will all spill out.

If the moon has a large ring at night, a snow storm is coming.

If the moon has a halo, the next day will be foggy.

If a rainbow forms during a shower, the weather will clear.

If there is a red sunset, rain will follow.

"A rainbow in the morning is a sailor's warning;
A rainbow at night is a sailor's delight."

SUPERSTITIONS ABOUT SNAKES

A dream that a rattlesnake has bitten you foretells bad luck.

A rattlesnake charms an animal before killing it for food.

A rattlesnake lying on its back will bring rain.

When rattlesnakes are restless, rain is coming.

The skin of a newly killed rattlesnake tied around the neck will prevent illness.   (Mexican superstition.)

Roadrunners kill rattlesnakes by building a wall of prickly pear around them.   (Mexican superstition.)

A person bitten by a rattlesnake over which birds are circling is not likely to die.

If you dream of a snake and a friend in the same night, the friend will die.

If you step upon a water snake, bad luck will follow.

If you kill the first snake you see in the spring, you will conquer all your enemies during the year; but if the snake gets away, the year will be filled with bad luck.

A snake killed during the day does not die until sundown.

The killing of a snake brings rain within three days.

Horsehairs put into rain water will turn into snakes.[1]

SUPERSTITIONS ABOUT CATS AND OTHER ANIMALS

If you swing a cat around by her tail, the direction in which her head points when she falls is the direction in which your sweetheart lives.

[1]This superstition dates back at least as far as Shakespeare's time:
"Which like the courser's hair, hath yet but life.
And not a serpent's poison."
    —*Antony and Cleopatra*, I, ii, 200.—Editor.

If a cat yells when she is held by the tail, her feet will point in the direction from which will come a letter telling of a death.

If a cat washes its face, company will come from the direction in which the tail points.

A cat washing her face knows that company is coming.

The tail of a sleeping cat points in the direction from which company will come.

If you keep a black cat for one year, you will have good luck for two years.

If a black cat comes to live with you, the best kind of luck will follow.

A black cat crossing the road will bring bad luck unless you turn back.

If a black and white cat crosses your path, you will have good luck.

If a white cat crosses your path, you will have good luck.

If you move away and leave a cat at the vacant house, you will have bad luck.

If you move a cat, you will have bad luck.

If a cat walks in front of you and meows, you will have bad luck.

If you kill a cat, you will have bad luck.

When a tomcat runs away, you will have bad luck.

If a horse becomes sick but the tail remains hard, the animal will not die.

If a cow falls down tail first, when she dies she will come to life again.

The devil's horse, or praying mantis, points toward Mecca with its head.

If a dog carries his tail between his legs, he will become mad.

If you succeed in counting the number of geese in a migratory flock, the birds will become confused and lose their places.

SOCIAL SUPERSTITIONS

If a rooster crows behind the back door, company will come.

If a rooster crows through a door or window, company is coming.

If a harvestman, or grandaddy, crawling up a wall goes in the direction you tell him, company will come from that direction.

If you drop a dishrag, company will come.

If your right hand itches, you will shake hands with a stranger.

If the palm of your hand itches, someone is talking about you.

When you right ear burns, someone is talking good about you, but when your left burns, someone is cursing you.

When your ear rings, someone is talking about you.

When your nose itches, company is coming.

If a fly sits upon your nose, someone wants to see you.

If you open and shut a pair of scissors in a roomful of company, everyone will begin to yawn.

If you get a hiccup, someone is thinking of you.

A hole in the stocking means a letter in the mail.

If you darn a stocking without taking it off, someone will tell a lie about you.

SUPERSTITIONS OF LOVE AND MARRIAGE

If a girl has someone name the corners of her room before she goes to bed, her future husband will have the name of the corner that she first sees when she gets up in the morning.

If you turn thirty-one rings with gems in them on the hands of thirty-one different girls, the last stone will be the color of the neckties your future husband wears.

If girls drink cold coffee at mealtimes, they will become beautiful.

A girl should never drink out of the spout of a coffee pot; if she does so, she will get a cross-eyed husband.

Count seven stars for seven nights, and on the last night you will dream of your lover.

A burning match held upright will twist until the end points to where your sweetheart lives.

If your hiccups stop while you are thinking of a girl's name, she will become your sweetheart.

Every time your shoe becomes untied your sweetheart is thinking of you.

If a girl loses a pin from her dress, she will lose her sweetheart.

If your stockings come down, your sweetheart will write to you.

A boy that picks up a rose dropped by a girl will become her sweetheart.

The toe of a stocking hung on a line will point toward your sweetheart's house.

If you chance to meet a girl twice in the same place, she will become your sweetheart.

If you wink at a girl, she will become your sweetheart.

If you drop your belt, the buckle will point toward your sweetheart's house.

If four persons shake hands across each other's arms, one of them will marry soon.

If you lose a gold ring and do not hunt for it, a girl will buy you another.

If the ends of a hairpin you find are even, you will see a new girl that day.

If the dog barks toward you, your girl will come to see you.

If you see a red-haired girl, you will see a grey horse; and if you see a grey horse, you will soon see a red-haired girl.

If an empty bottle is spun in a circle of girls, the open end will point toward the one that will marry first.

If a boy walks under a horseshoe hanging over the door, the girl living in the house will marry him.

If you spill ink on a letter to your friend, he will marry soon.

If you drop your fork, you will get another wife.

If the wedding day dawns clear, the marriage will be happy; if the day is cloudy and stormy, the married life will be likewise.

If you build a fire and it does not burn, your wife will be as ugly as mud.

For every white spot on your fingernails you will have a sweetheart.

For every star that a girl counts on her wedding night she will have a child.

If an old maid drops a hairpin in a cave, she will marry before the year is over.

If a broom falls upon the floor, the girl that steps over it without picking it up will become an old maid.

If a girl pricks her finger with a pin, she will get a kiss.

SIGNS PREDICTING DEATH

A run-away mule means death in the family.

If the dog howls at midnight, you will have bad luck or a death in the family.

If a hen crows like a rooster, someone in the family will die.

If a bird flies very near you, there will be a death in the family.

If a woodpecker taps on the roof of the house, someone in it will die.

If a pet dies and you cry over it, someone in the family will die.

If the peach blossoms are red, you will have a friend die.

If the sun casts a red light upon a house in the evening, someone in that house will die.

If the sun is red when it sinks, somebody's blood is there.

If rain falls during a funeral, one of those present will die soon.

If three men light their cigars from the same match, one of them will die.

If a Mexican dies, his family must move away immediately.

Never take off a wedding ring, for that means that one of the couple will die.

If you dream that you have lost all of your teeth, there will be a death in the family soon.

To have an old house remodeled brings death.

If you carry a hoe in one door and out the other, some member of the family will die.

Clean your shoes before returning from a funeral. Not to do so means a death in the family.

If the chimney of a lamp is broken and the flame continues to burn, there will be a death in the family.

If wet clothes hang out on New Year's night, there will be a death in the family during the coming year.

OMENS OF MISFORTUNE OTHER THAN DEATH

To return for something that was forgotten brings bad luck.

Always enter a house through the same door by which you left; else bad luck will follow.

Never open an umbrella in the house, for bad luck will follow.

If an ax is carried through the house, you will have bad luck.

A rake on the ground with the prongs up brings bad luck.

A knife given as a present to a friend will cut that friendship unless something is given in exchange.

If you drop a knife, you will have bad luck.

If you drop your fork during a meal, you must not finish that meal lest bad luck get you.

When a pair of scissors falls on the ground and sticks upright, bad luck will come.

If you do not want to take a cup along but do so anyway, the cup will break.

A broken mirror brings seven years of bad luck.

If a stocking is put on backwards in the morning, it must be worn so the rest of the day; else bad luck will come.

If you put on one stocking backwards, put the other on likewise to keep the witches away.

If you do not stop the motion of a rocking-chair when you get up, bad luck will follow.

If the fire in the stove roars, stir it well; else there will be a quarrel in the family.

Do not tell a secret in a room, for the walls have ears and will repeat it when you are gone.

If you sweep after six o'clock, you will have bad luck.

When your right hand itches, you will pay out some money.

Before passing a bow-legged man, spit in your hat and walk past on the left side.

If you spit on more than three horseshoes in one day, you will have bad luck.

Bad luck will get you if the wind blows off your hat.

If the full moon shines in a person's face while he sleeps, he will walk in his sleep.

Do not watch departing guests, for to do so will bring bad luck.

If two friends pass on opposite sides of a tree, they will quarrel soon unless they say "bread and butter" as they pass.

If you see a red-haired girl that is cross-eyed, take three steps backward and turn around before passing her.

Never thank a person for flower cuttings until they begin to grow; else they will die.

Never plant parsley seed directly into the ground, for bad luck will get you. Always scatter the seed upon the kitchen floor and throw it out with the sweepings. The plants will grow then.

If a rabbit runs across your path in a field, you must avoid the trail, for misfortune walks upon it.

A black butterfly that follows a person will bring bad luck.

"A spider at night brings delight.
A spider in the morning is a gypsy's warning."

When a dog whines, you will have bad luck.

When your dog whines, you will have a sick friend.

If the chickens lay abnormally small eggs, a member of the family will become ill for each egg laid.

If you break a very small egg laid by your hens, you will have bad luck.

Baby chickens hatched in April will die.

If you are on your way to do business with someone and a bird crosses your path, you must turn back, for you will have no success that day.

If a bird flies into the house, you will have bad luck.

When a blackbird sings near you, bad luck will come.

To kill a blackbird is to invite bad luck.

The shadow of a buzzard crossing your path brings bad luck.

Never disturb an owl that sits between you and the moon. To do so will bring bad luck.

A bird that sings before breakfast will be eaten by the cat.

Children that sing before breakfast will be taken by the devil.

If children sing before breakfast, there will be a quarrel in the family.

A bad dream told before breakfast will come true.

If a child crawls through the window, it will not grow any more.

"Comb your hair after dark, comb sorrow to your heart."

If you drop your comb, have someone else pick it up, for if you pick it up you will have misfortune.

Do not move on Friday.

Friday the thirteenth is an unlucky day.

Thirteen is an unlucky number and three is lucky.

The ghosts decide whether a negro will go to heaven or to hell.

If a negro is burned, he will go to hell.

GOOD LUCK SIGNS

If you meet a white horse and a red-haired girl, you will have good luck.

If a girl's dress is turned up at the hem, she will get a new dress.

If a girl puts on her dress backwards, she will get a new one.

If a woman sleeps with her gown backwards until midnight and then changes it, she will have good luck.

If you find a horseshoe, spit on it and throw it over your shoulder; then if you do not watch where it falls, you will have good luck.

If you hang up a horseshoe, you will have good luck.

A horseshoe on a post brings good luck.

A horseshoe hung in a fruit tree will make the tree bear and prevent its freezing.[2]

If a bug gets on a girl, she will get a dress the color of the bug.

A toad in the garden brings good luck.

A chirping cricket brings good luck.

If a butterfly sits on your hat, you will get a new hat.

If you see a redbird, make a wish.

If you see a dead bird, make a wish and it will come true.

The foot of a rabbit that has been killed by a cross-eyed negro on the night of the full moon at twelve o'clock in a cemetery near the grave of a bad man will work as a charm against evil.[3]

If you carry a potato in your pocket, your rheumatism will leave as soon as the potato is shriveled up.

If you cut an apple seed in two, your wish made then will be granted.

If you find some money and do not spend it, you will have good luck.

---

[2]I have seen three or four horseshoes hung upon a single fruit tree in Fredericksburg, Gillespie County, where the population is chiefly German. In some instances the tree has grown entirely over the arch of a horseshoe placed long ago at a fork.—Editor.

[3]This superstition, like many another, seems to have originated in a spirit of ironic humor.—Editor.

If you see a fire in the pasture, you will find a pot of gold buried there.

Hair pins hung on the fence bring good luck.

If you see a pin with the point toward you, pick it up for good luck.

"See a pin and pick it up,
  And that little act will bring good luck."

If you pull an eyebrow hair and give it to a friend and then guess on which finger the friend puts it, your wish will come true.

To have good luck you should put your left shoe on first.

If your left arm itches, you will get some money.

Look over your right shoulder at the new moon to bring good luck. Look over your left shoulder and you will have bad luck.

A child born on Sunday can see into the future.

Dreams dreamed on Saturday night will come true.

If you make a wish before a falling star fades away, the wish will come true.

If a tooth is pulled and the tongue is not put where it grew, a gold tooth will come in its place.

Carry a new broom, a piece of bread, and some salt into a new house for good luck.

If rain falls on or in a new grave, the person buried there will go to heaven. (Negro superstition.)

A gold ring hung over a glass of water so that it just touches the surface will dip into the water as many times as the years of your life.

WART CURES

If an onion is rubbed on a wart and then buried, the wart will leave.

A piece of raw meat rubbed on a wart will cause it to leave.

If a wart is rubbed with a piece of potato, which is then thrown over the house, the wart will disappear.

If you rub an old dishrag over your wart and then bury it under the back steps without anyone's knowing of it, your wart will leave.

If the wart is rubbed with a piece of bacon, which is then buried where the water from the eaves can drip on it, the wart will leave as soon as the bacon rots.

If a string is tied around a wart and then buried, the wart will disappear.

If milk is poured on a wart, it will leave.

A wart can be cured by putting the milk from the milkweed on it.

If you spit on a wart before getting up, it will leave.

Throw a bone over your left shoulder and the warts will leave.

If you take a dead black cat to the cemetery at midnight and leave the cat there without anyone's knowing it, your warts will leave.

If you say to the full moon, "Full moon, please take my warts away," the warts will leave.

BUFFALO LORE AND BOUDIN BLANC

By Douglas Branch

When Nathaniel Southgate Shaler[1] dug around the salt springs at Big Bone Lick, Kentucky, he found ten feet below the surface and extending to an unknown depth, the remains of great elephants, their skeletons broken into pieces by the tread of successive generations. Above that level lay the remains of a musk-ox, once forced into this southern country by the march of the great glacier, together with the remains of a long-extinct species of bison. After these animals had passed away, after smaller game had come to the springs and sunk in the mire and their kind had been forgotten, came the buffalo.

There were Indians west of the Rockies before there were buffaloes. By the story of the Apaches, that tribe, after it had emerged from Un-go-ya-yen-ni, the underworld, had no food except flour ground from plant-seeds—until the coming of the buffalo.[2] And if, in Pawnee lore, the buffalo was not included in the assemblies of animals, the Na-hu-rak lodges, it must have been because the buffalo was a late-comer.

The Cheyennes told that before the coming of the buffalo the Indian people lived at the head of a stream—in the Llano Estacado, most likely—that emptied into a cave. One time they were nearly starving, and decided to explore the cave. Three Indians went in; and at last they came to a door. An old woman opened it at their knocking, and asked what they wanted. They said that they and their people were starving. The old woman gave them buffalo meat to eat, and when they went back they found the whole prairie covered with buffaloes. Then the three braves led the Cheyennes in their first buffalo hunt. Most of the Plains accounts are variations on this theme.

In 1879 Stone Calf, the Cheyenne chief, told Colonel Dodge that buffaloes were produced in countless numbers under the ground, that every spring their surplus swarmed out of great

[1]N. S. Shaler, *Nature and Man in America* (1891).

[2]Frank Russell, "Myths of the Jicarilla Apaches," *Journal of American Folklore*, XI, p. 260.

cave-like openings to this country; that the Great Spirit had provided the buffalo for the constant food of the Indian, and that, however recklessly the white men might slaughter the buffaloes, they could never exterminate them. But when in 1885 a young army surgeon spoke to Stone Calf about the buffalo, he was very much troubled: the Evil Spirits had closed up the mouth of the cave and the buffaloes could not get out. He and Chief Little Robe wanted to go to Washington and get permission from the Great Father to open the cave and let the buffaloes out.[3]

The northern Indians located the home of the buffalo in their own country, under a lake far out in the prairie southwest of the Eagle Hills. "You say," said the mythical Red Man of a Canadian narrator,[4] "they are all gone; but look, they come again and again to us. We cannot kill them all—they are under that lake. Do you hear the noise which never ceases? It is the buffalo fighting with each other far down under the ground, and striving to get out on the prairie—where else can they come from?"

The account of the Skidi Pawnee is more elaborate. George A. Dorsey was told: "At the creation of all things, Ti-wa-ra made a buffalo to stand in the north, which was to be the home of the buffalo. The buffalo was given a mate. Here they increased, so that when the buffalo became old, it was given a place to stand at the north entrance where the heavens touch the earth, where it was to pass in and out whomever Ti-wa-ra wished to send out and call in. For many years the buffalo was standing at this place, and each year it would drop off some of its hairs, so that when all the hair had dropped off from it, the world should come to an end. This buffalo was the father of all the buffalo."[5] The buffaloes became numerous; it was cold in the north; there was not much grass. But a Spider-Woman ruled over the center of the earth, and she would not let them pass. Then the buffaloes tried strategy; they asked her for some tobacco, to divert her attention. But she would not let them come near her. Then the chief of the

---

[3]R. I. Dodge, *Our Wild Indians* (1883); C. C. McNary, in correspondence section of *Adventure* Magazine, Dec. 20, 1923.

[4]W. F. Butler, *The Wild North Land* (1874).

[5]G. A. Dorsey, *Traditions of the Skidi Pawnee* (1904), p. 36.

buffaloes gave orders that his kind should trample over Spider-Woman and her fields, "and scatter the seeds all over the earth, that they might grow, and that the people might gather them and get their seeds from there." So the buffaloes knocked down her cobwebs, and rushed past the center of the earth; and "the people everywhere obtained buffalo, where they had not been known."

For the Plains Indians the buffalo was the answer to the terrible necessity of getting food. Without it their existence might have been little better than the precarious, abject living of the Shoshone Diggers; about it they built a culture. Buffalo was their most common food. The robe was the Indian's winter covering and his bed; the dressed skin was his summer blanket. Shirts, leggings, women's dresses, quivers, bow-cases, and moccasins, sheaths, parfleches for carrying, were all made of the buffalo skin. Ropes were made of braided rawhide or twisted hair. Dressed skins made the Indian's house. The hoofs of the buffalo were boiled for glue to fasten heads and feathers to arrows; the sinews were used for bow-strings and for backing for the bows.[6] All this is common knowledge; but in this day of a literature of escape the intimate every-day importance of the buffalo to the Indian must be emphasized to explain the extreme emphasis placed on it in Indian legend and ritual. "The Blackfeet ask, 'What one of all animals is most sacred? And the reply given is, 'The buffalo.' "[7]

John Bradbury, near an Aricara camp on the upper Sioux, found on a bluff fourteen buffalo skulls placed in a row; he learned that the arrangement was intended as an honor to the buffaloes the Indians had killed, to placate them so they would not warn the living buffaloes of the coming of the Indians on their next hunt. In a world of such ever-presence of life the buffaloes had much to do besides wait in legend for some semi-mythical hero to slay them; always they were Power, or Food, or both.

Before a great hunt came the buffalo-dance. Of the numerous accounts of men who knew the Plains Indians, that of

---

[6]For a suggestion of the many minor uses of the buffalo, see David I. Bushnell, Jr., "The Various Uses of Buffalo Hair by the North American Indians," *The American Anthropologist*, II (July, 1909), pp. 401-425.

[7]G. B. Grinnell, "The Last of the Buffalo," *Scribner's*, XII (Sept., 1892), p. 267.

Prince Maximilian, who in the early eighteen-thirties witnessed the Manitari ritual for the winter hunt, best suggests the earthiness of it. ("Through the corn and the buffalo we worship the Great Father.") The utter sincerity of the appeal for food is unmistakable; the appeal *must* be heard.

Six elderly men had been chosen to represent buffalo bulls. Each carried a medicine stick, with one end ornamented with the hoofs of buffalo calves. Two had drums. They "rattled their sticks incessantly, sang alternately, and imitated, with great perfection, the hoarse voice of the buffalo bull." Dishes of boiled maize and beans were passed around by provision-bearers, each man tasting a small quantity; and dishes were also passed and tasted that were then empty but that soon might hold buffalo meat. There followed speeches of "good wishes for success in hunting the buffalo, and in war." Then came the passing of the pipes. "The pipe bearers often turned their pipes toward the cardinal points, and performed various superstitious manoeuvres with them." The six buffalo bulls, meantime, sitting behind the fire, sang and rattled the medicine sticks, while one of them constantly beat the badger skin. "After a while they all stood up, bent forward, and danced; that is, they leaped as high as they could with both their feet together, continuing to sing and rattle their sticks, one of them beating time on the badger. Their song was invariably the same, consisting of loud, broken notes and exclamations."

Later, "when the ceremony had continued a couple of times, the women began to act their part. A woman approached her husband, gave him her girdle and under garment, so she had nothing on under her robe; she then went to one of the most distinguished men, passed her hand over his arm, from the shoulder downwards, and then withdrew slowly from the lodge. The person so summoned follows her to a solitary place in the forest; he may buy himself off by presents, which, however, few Indians do." Maximilian adds, "This honour was offered to us, but we returned to the lodge, after having made a present." The Manitari ceremony always continued for four successive days.[8]

After the hunt most of the Plains tribes made some gesture

[8]Prince Maximilian, "Travels," in Thwaites' *Early Western Travels*, XXIV, pp. 28-31.

of sacrifice. A traditional form required a pious hunter to decide upon one particular buffalo to be sacrificed; ultimately, it seems, the meat fell to the shamans; the flesh was carried to the shamans' house packed in a prescribed way, and as the horse stood before the lodge to be unloaded, the head of the buffalo he carried pointed to the north, the old home of the species.

With the Crow Indians a white buffalo, a great rarity that even the Great Spirit must notice, was marked for an offering. When a Crow discovered a white buffalo he promised it to the sun. If he succeeded in his kill, he left it untouched: "Take her; she is yours."

But with the Mandans the skin of a white buffalo was fine medicine. The hide must be that of a young cow, and must be taken off complete, with the horns, nose, hoofs, and tail attached. Neighboring tribes profited by this Mandan belief, for a good white skin would bring the price of ten or fifteen horses. Once a Mandan obtained such a skin, he engaged a medicine man, who must walk about the village in the direction of the sun's course and sing a medicine song. "When the owner, after collecting articles of value for three or four years"—to return to Maximilian—"desires to offer up his treasure to the lord of life, or to the first man, he rolls it up, after adding some wormwood or a head of maize, and the skin then remains suspended on a high pole until it rots away."

Buffalo-lore itself may be casually divided into myths of culture-origins, legends of conflict, and legends of transformation. In the stories of conflict the buffalo has a paradoxical role: sometimes he is the vanquished opponent of a tribal hero, and again he befriends some poor man whom the tribe despises, giving him great magic. There are stories of buffaloes who appear as people and are accepted into the tribe, and stories of men who are turned into buffaloes.

The Ojibwa story of the great man Me-je-we-dah is both a hero-story and a transformation-story. Me-je-we-dah told his braves not to say anything to a certain animal they would meet, as the animal would understand and be angry. About noon they saw this animal—a buffalo; and one foolish brave said that this buffalo was nothing to be afraid of. "The buffalo knew in himself that this foolish fellow was not afraid of him. So after the braves knew the buffalo was angry they all stood in one row. The buffalo came up to the foolish brave, who then turned and fled, but the buffalo ran him down." Then the foolish brave turned into a partridge, but the buffalo turned into a bird and pursued him. The brave then turned back into a man; the buffalo turned into a man, too, and ran him down again. The brave jumped into a little lake and turned into a fish; the buffalo-man grabbed a spear and soon speared the fish. He threw it to the party of braves; and when it dropped, it was the brave again—"only he was dead." The buffalo-man assumed his original form, but he was still angry. Me-je-we-dah was angry now, too; they charged each other, and Me-je-we-dah took hold of the buffalo's horns and killed him by splitting his head open.[9]

George Bird Grinnell's re-telling of Ti-ke-wa-kush, the Man Who Called the Buffalo, is a peculiarly desultory legend that must have acquired its half-dozen incidents in a manner to be suggested later. One of these incidents, the first, starts the tale in the grand manner: "This happened in the olden time before we met the white people." There was famine. "The children cried and the women cried; they had nothing at all to eat. There was a person who looked at the children crying for something to eat, and it touched his heart." Because he could call the buffaloes to him, the tribe was saved. "After four days, as they were going out to surround the buffalo for the third time, the wind changed, and before the people got near them the buffalo smelt them, and stampeded. While they were galloping away, the man ran up to the top of the hill, to the place of sacrifice, carrying a pole, on which was tied the skin of a kit fox; and when he saw the buffalo running, and that the people could not catch them, he waved his pole and called out *Ska-a-a-a!* and the buffalo turned right about, and charged right back through the people, killing many of them. He wished to show the people that he had power over the buffalo."[10] Incidentally, in this heroic Pawnee legend, as Mr. Grinnell himself has pointed out, lies the shadow of a recollection that the Pawnee tribe hunted on foot before the

---

[9]Harlan I. Smith, "Some Ojibwa Myths and Traditions," *Journal of American Folklore*, XIX, p. 221.

[10]Grinnell, *Pawnee Hero Stories* (1916).

coming of the wild horses, and actually used a human decoy who "called" the buffaloes.

Another origin-story, that cannot be explained away by the academicians as simply an instance of primitive rationalizing, is the Dakota tale of Coyote, the "culture-hero." Once Coyote was walking along. He was hungry, thin, and weak. Finally he came upon a knife and an arrow. He carried them away with him, and after a while found a valley full of buffaloes. He took the arrow and threw it toward the buffaloes, saying, "Now, go and kill the buffalo. Go, hit that one." But the arrow said, "You must take a piece of wood and string before I can hit the buffalo." Coyote made a bow, and after more trials that failed, used it rightly. "The arrow flew towards the buffalo, struck one of them in the side, but did not bring it down. Coyote picked up the knife and ran after the wounded buffalo as fast as he could. He shouted so loud that the wounded buffalo soon fell over from fright." Then he butchered the animal.[11]

"The flesh of the buffalo was the most wholesome, palatable, and universally used" of all animal flesh. The Indian despised the "insipid lard" of the domestic cow; but his stomach never rebelled against buffalo-fat. The marrow, the liver, and the small intestines were to be eaten just at the close of the hunt; the tongue and the hump were delicacies for the evening's celebration; and the meat, mixed with fat into pemmican, or sliced thin and dried by the sun or fire, was provision for those seasons when there were no buffaloes.

Buffalo was also Power; and the Querechos and Tejas Indians, wrote Pedro de Castenada, "open the belly of a cow . . . squeeze out the chewed grass and drink the juice that remains behind, because they say that this contains the strength of the stomach"—the courage, the endurance, the obstinacy of the buffalo.

To go further into this gourmanderie, to explain how the Sioux made soup of buffalo meat, corn, and bear's oil, and clamored with the dogs for more than their share; how marrow-fat was skimmed and boiled and clarified into a rich golden mass to be packed in buffalo-bladders; how tongues

---

[11]Clark Wissler, "Some Dakota Myths," *Journal of American Folklore,* XX, p. 124.

were steeped in cold, then in tepid water, soaked in brine for
a half-month, and dry-smoked; how your true Indian tore the
liver from the scarcely-killed buffalo, dipped it into the gall,
and ate; how the hump was roasted under cinders and earth—
would be to compile a futile *Physiologie du Gout.* But if the
boudin blanc is understood, then the buffalo-tales of the Plains
Indians will hold only minor mysteries. Captain Meriwether
Lewis, in his immortal *Journal,* described this native American
dish:

"From the buffalo cow I killed we saved the necessary
materials for making what our wrighthand cook Charbono
calls the *boudin (poudinge) blanc,* and immediately set him
about preparing them for supper; this white pudding we all
esteem one of the greatest delicacies of the forest. . . . About
six feet of the lower extremity of the large gut of the Buffaloe
is the first morsel that the cook makes love to, this he holds
fast at one end with the right hand, while with the forefinger
and thumb of his left he gently compresses it and discharges
what he says *is not good to eat,* but of which in the sequal
we get a moderate portion; the mustle lying beneath the
shoulder blade to the back, and fillets are next saught, these
are needed up very fine with a good portion of kidney suit;
to this composition is then added a just proportion of pepper
and salt and a small quantity of flour; thus far advanced, our
skilfull operator C———o seizes his receptacle, which has never
once touched water, for that would intirely distroy the regular
order of the whole procedure; you will not forget that this
side you see now is that covered with a good coat of fat provided the animal be in good order; the opporater sceizes the
receptacle I say, and tying it fast at one end turns it inward
and begins anew with repeated evolutions of the hand and arm,
and a brisk motion of his finger and thumb to put in what
he says is *bon pour manger;* thus by stuffing and compressing
he soon distends the receptacle to the utmost limits of it's
power of expansion . . . thus when the sides of the receptacle
are skilfully exchanged the outer for the inner . . . it is tied
at the end, but not any cut off, for that would make the pattern too scant; it is then baptised in the missouri with two
dips and a flirt, and bobbed into the kettle; from whence,
after it be well boyled it is **taken and** fryed with bears oil
untill it becomes brown. . . ."

One classic leads to another. Washington Irving, in *Captain Bonneville,* wrote of the Captain's most pleasant encounter with the Bannock Indians: "Some men are said to wax valorous on a full stomach, and such seemed to be the case with the Banneck braves, who, in proportion as they crammed themselves with buffalo meat, grew stout of heart, until, the supper at an end, they began to chant war songs, setting forth their mighty deeds and the victories they had gained over the Blackfeet. Warming with the theme, and inflating themselves with their own eulogies, these magnanimous heroes of the trencher would start up, advance a short distance beyond the light of the fire, and apostrophize most vehemently their Blackfeet enemies, as though they had been within hearing."

But under such happy circumstances there was not always talk of war; sometimes there must have been talk of the food—the buffalo.

Anthropologists have long—and sometimes curiously—accounted for the clouded origins of legends by endowing primitive folk with a perpetual perplexity, reading into every tale either rhapsodized history or a puzzled inquiry into Ti-ra-wh-hut, the Universe-and-Everything-Inside. But many of these buffalo tales have the smack of banqueters whose food lies heavy on their stomachs, whose time is heavy on their hands.

John R. Swanton has preserved a fine tale of the Alabama and Kosati Indians: "There was an old woman who lived with her grand-daughter. One time she sent her grand-daughter with a bucket to a pond to get some water. When the girl had dipped her water out, she set it down and stood up. Then she saw an old buffalo come to the other side of the pond. It called to her to come over, and she went away with it. Then the girl's people did not know where she had gone, and they hunted for her everywhere. They promised a trunk full of things to the person who could tell where she had gone; but no one knew. By and by a poor man said, 'I will go hunting for her, and find her.' 'All right,' they said. 'Hunt for her and bring her back.' Before the man started off, however, he made four arrows, two of which were red and two white. He also took along four hen's eggs. After he had travelled for a while, he came to a place where there

were many buffalo, and in the very middle sat a girl. Then
the poor man climbed up into a post-oak tree the head of which
bent far over, and he tried to put the animals to sleep. After
a while, all fell asleep but one old buffalo, who walked around
continually. At last he went to sleep also. Then the man
got down from his tree quickly, seized the girl, and dragged
her to the tree against her will, for she did not want to go.
When he got nearly there, all of the buffalo woke up and
pursued him; but he carried the girl up into the tree and
placed himself just above her. Immediately they were surrounded by the buffalo. Then the buffalo began licking the
tree, and they licked it until they very nearly made it fall over.
The man, however, took one of the eggs he had brought, and
dropped it on the ground, and the tree stood erect as before.
. . . He did this four times. Then he took one of his red
arrows and began shooting at the buffalo. After every shot,
the arrow returned to him again; and he kept on in this way
until all of the buffalo, except the old one, had been killed.
The buffalo, however, began kicking pine-knots up at his
opponent; and the man would take these and throw them
back. This went on for some time, until finally the man drew
a red arrow again, and shot the buffalo so that he dropped
dead. When the woman saw this, she cried, jumped down
out of the tree, and threw herself upon the old buffalo's body.
The man cut out the tongues of all the buffalo, and said to
the woman, 'Let us go.' She would not; so he took away all
of her clothes, and killed her. Then he went home and
showed the clothes to her people. All came together, and
gave him the trunk full of things that had been promised."[12]

This is more than a legend; it is a genuine after-dinner
story. Perhaps it is the epic of a tribal migration, in cipher;
but it is also irresistible nonsense born of a satisfaction with
living.

The story of the falling of the last hairs of the Father of
the Buffalo, of the ending of the world of the Plains Indians,
is the account of the collapse of a mythology. The slaughter-
ing of the buffalo (with the Department of the Interior the
unctuous chief mourner and chief accomplice) was an insult

---

[12]J. R. Swanton, "Animal Stories from the Indians of the Muskhogean
Stock," *Journal of American Folklore*, XXVI, p. 212.

to Ti-wa-ra; and if there was a Ti-wa-ra, he did not answer.

Julian Ralph, in Calgary in 1889, learned that some Indians "now take their ponies in the springtime and ride away as of old, but in silence and sadness.

" 'Where are you bound?' some white man inquires.

" 'For the buffalo,' is the reply.

" 'But there are no more.'

" 'No, we know it.'

" 'Then why are you going on such a foolish chase?'

" 'Oh, we always go at this time; maybe we shall find some.' "

But that generation of Indians is dead; and the descendants of the Plains Indians are today stodgy Methodists or stodgy agnostics, and they have little to tell. For anyone who cares to follow the buffalo through Indian folk-lore George A. Dorsey's *Legends of the Skidi Pawnee,* Mr. Grinnell's *Pawnee Hero Stories and Folk Tales,* and Frances Densmore's *The Teton Sioux* are an easily accessible beginning. After that will come the thumbing of ethnological reports and of folk-lore society publications; and beyond these the seeker will occasionally discover a fine morsel of a tale in an unexpected place, sweetening some yellowing volume of Western Americana.

OLD TIME DARKY PLANTATION MELODIES

By Natalie Taylor Carlisle

As many Southerners have observed, the old time darky's trusting religious faith, his loyalty to his daily tasks, his love for "ole marse" and "ole mist'ess," and his richly flavored sayings make a very attractive memory. My own memories do not go back to slave days, but on the plantation of my relatives in Franklin County, North Carolina, and on my own plantation in Washington County, Texas, I have known well the old fashioned negro. Further, I grew up hearing my father tell tales of the darkies on his parents' plantation in Wake Forest County, North Carolina. Uncle Caesar, Daddy Arp, Dancin' Jinny, Wellington, and Washington, who lived to be 102 years old, were favorite characters in his reminiscence. Most of the material that follows is taken from the negroes of Washington County, Texas.

People who live next to the soil are usually mellow with human philosophy, and nothing more characterized the old time darky than his saws and maxims. Many of them he jubilated in singing; others he mulled over and iterated with all the gusto of his healthy nature. Like the wisdom of Solomon, the wisdom of these saws and maxims is a natural wisdom, a kindly wisdom. I quote a few of them that I have never heard sung:

"Whatever goes over the old devil's back slides back under his belly."

"Whar dey ain't no devils, dey ain't no need fer angels."

"Ever' time a fine, prancin' horse gits a shoe, a pesky little hoppin' frog puts up his foot fer the same reward."

"De spirit can sing, but de flesh must wail."

"A spry tongue makes a doleful way."

"A keerful tongue makes a happy heart."

"Yer mustn't stretch out yer feet longer 'n yer blanket."

"A pu'son widout teeth can find gladness in a soup bowl."

"When de cock crows three times yer better be up and doin'."

"A dew fer three mornin's brings a rain."

In such a song as "Friendship Am Golden," the darky sums
up into an aphorism his philosophy of friendship.

Friendship am golden, friendship am golden,
Oh, friendship am golden, I say.
Keep yo' hand on yo' pocket-book,
Caze dat am yo' friend.
Keep yo' hand on yo' pocket-book,
Dat's golden.

It is said that some "white brethern" have so admired the text
of this song that a popular ballad has been written expressing
its sentiment.

Something like a song maxim, also, is "Religion Is a Fortune."

Oh, religion is a fortune, I really do believe.
Oh, religion is a fortune, I really do believe.
Where has you been, poor sinner, where has you been so long?
You ought ter walk and talk wid Jesus,
I really do believe.

I's gwine to chatter wid de angels, I really do believe.
I's gwine to chatter wid de angels, I really do believe.
Where has you been, poor sinner, where has you been so long?
Oh, come and walk and talk wid Jesus,
And den you will believe.

The subject matter of the old time negro's song was a part
of his daily experiences. Furthermore, his peculiar style of
music was part and parcel of himself. Whatever he experi-
enced he sang. Most of his songs had few words because most
of them centered upon a single idea or circumstance. However, the song itself might be as long as the individual singer
wished to make it, the length depending entirely upon the
mood and occupation of the singer and not upon the number
of words in it. Sometimes a song was an entire day's length.
The following, a great favorite in past times, is said to have
had its origin in a path along a river-side where there were
both sand and clay-mud. In walking along this path, which
led from plantation quarters to a negro church, the church
people constantly warned each other to keep out of the mud
and to stay in the sand. From this warning grew the song:

Take 'em out de mud,
Keep yo' foot in de sand.

After being sung in this order for a long time, the song used
to be reversed and sung thus:

Keep it in de sand,
Take yo' foot out de mud.

I have heard the song sung at such length that at night, when
all became still, the words and melody would echo on in
dreams and it would seem that all things alive on the plantation—horses, mules, cows, cats, dogs, fowls, and all the darkies
—had gathered together in one grand and supreme chorus
and were singing,

Take it out de mud,
Keep yo' foot in de sand.

Thus a song of very few words might become very, very long.

A favorite song to charm away the time while splitting wood was this:

Oh, Lord, de wood am hard an' de ax am dull.
Oh, Lordy, help dis nigger.

The old time wood chopper sang steadily and puffed between the strokes of the ax. Had it been suggested that he might chop more comfortably if he would not sing, his reply would have been that singing "warmed him up" and made work easier. If the chopper was feeling particularly energetic, the song had a different version, running thus:

Oh, Lord, de wood am hard,
But de ax am sharp.
How de Lord do help dis nigger!

There are persons who contend that negro melodies are not melodies at all, but that they are simply moanings, wailings, or croonings. It must be conceded that some of the melodies do have a distinctly wailing sound. From a musical point of view a melody is a succession of musical tones rhythmical and pleasing to the ear. None can deny that the darky melodies are successions of musical tones capable of being played out on any musical instrument; and even though the rhythm may change two or three times in one short song, the rhythm does exist. Is it pleasing to the ear? Emphatically, yes. The melody is fascinating.

A particular motif that runs through most of these melodies is the interval of the fourth, both ascending and descending, in the bolder or sustained notes; and the intervals of the second and third in the shorter notes, ascending and descending. These motifs are constantly employed, but in such a variety of arrangement as to make different melodies.

In the following song, which shows the negro's fidelity in

religion, as in the wood chopper's song also, there are the fourth interval on the bold notes and the second and third intervals on the short notes, the arrangement being such that the melodies are very different, though the darky "song color" is immediately recognizable in each.

I's yose, oh, Lord, an' I won't turn back.
No, Lord, I won't turn back!

Ef de whole world go back on me,
Oh, Lord, I won't turn back!

Ef my mother go back on me,
No, Lord, I won't turn back!

A stanza is accorded to each member of the family relationship, and one even includes the preacher.

Ef my preacher go back on me,
I won't turn back, Lord!
No, I won't turn back!

An entirely different melody is found in the song of an old horse named "Joe" that continually kicked out of the harness. This song employs every note in the musical scale, in order descending, and forms a very gay melody.

Ole Joe! Ole Joe kickin' up behind and befo',
And de yaller gal a-kickin' up behind ole Joe!

This type of song, using as it does every note of the scale in succession, is very unusual among darky melodies; and when future generations delve back into the past for something fresh and "spicy," such a song as "Old Joe" will no doubt be prized as a musical gem of folk days.

Another gay melody, which was and perhaps still is particularly popular at cotton picking time, is called "Sallie's Red Dress." During cotton picking season cash is more plentiful than at any other time and thoughts then naturally turn to bright, new clothing. It will be noticed that "Sallie's Red Dress" again brings into evidence the intervals of the fourth, and of the second and third; yet it is very lightsome and not at all like some other songs that contain the characteristic intervals. Imagine this song as floating out on the warm, sunny air over the white fields of cotton in chorus exhilarant.

Oh, oh! you can't shine!   Oh, oh! you can't shine!
Oh, oh! you can't shine! Sallie's got a red dress
Buttoned behind!   Sallie's got a red dress
Buttoned behind!

The next two songs have been somewhat spoiled by modern efforts to publish them; they are given here in their original form. They express that simple and sincere religious trust that in the old time darky was combined with superstition. While they are amusing, in a degree, to the educated mind, it must be admitted that they carry an excellent point of view and even offer good advice.

> You better mind, oh, you better mind!
> Sister, you better mind how you talk.
> You better mind what you talkin' about,
> Caze you gotter give account o' yo'self at de judgment.
>
> Brother, you better mind how you pray.
> Preacher, you better mind what you preachin' about,
> Caze you gotter give account o' yo'self at de judgment.

"What Shall I Do?" shows the self rebuke of the contrite darky.

Oh, poor gambler, get down on yo' knees.
Oh, long-tongue liar, get down on yo' knees.
Oh, backslider from God, get down on yo' knees.
Oh, my Lordy, what shall I do?

The last song that I shall give shows the sentimental sus-
ceptibilities of the young darky to the charms of his lady love.
He can withstand the hardships of the weather and other
trials but cannot trust himself to the wiles of his "pretty gal."

Rain, come wet me;
Sun, come dry me;
Keep away, pretty gal;
Don't come a-nigh me.

The foregoing songs are within themselves a delineation of
the old time faithful, trusting, and to-be-trusted darky—the
darky that has almost passed and that has already become a
subject for history and folk-lore.

THE NEGRO AS INTERPRETER OF HIS OWN FOLK-SONGS[1]

BY R. C. HARRISON

As artist, as critic, and as interpreter of his own genius in other ways, the American Negro is achieving in the present decade his second emancipation, and further recorders of American literary history will have to give a long chapter to the achievement. Though this emancipation is primarily literary, the Negro has undoubtedly come into a new freedom in other ways of artistic expression. The process has been coextensive with the period since the Civil War, and fortunately has been accomplished without the dire results which attended the political upheaval of two generations ago; yet the Negro's advance towards an autocthonous literature has not been without desperate struggle. The greatest impediment to advancement has come from the two hundred and fifty years of political bondage that weighed upon the Negro up to the close of the Civil War. The second greatest hindering force has been racial prejudice, which was intensified, if not engendered, by the conclusion of the Civil War, and which has been directed towards the Negro ever since. A third impediment has been the tardiness with which the country, especially the white and black races of the South, has responded to the need of educating the liberated Negro. Other reasons for the Negro's tardy winning of a significant place in American literature are dependent on those just mentioned.

A little later I shall come to a brief discussion of the advance of the Negro as an interpreter of his own folk-lore. But let me first run over sixty years of the Negro's efforts to liberate himself from the literary bondage in which he has lived since obtaining his political freedom in 1865.

The first aspect is the rise during that time of the intellectual level of the Negro. Its most conspicuous manifestations

---

[1]This article was prepared before I had access to the recently published *Mellows* by R. E. Kennedy and *The New Negro* by Alain Locke. Both of these books are authoritative and both seem to me to strengthen my conclusions.

have been concerned with the achievements of such schools as Fisk University, Hampton Institute, Tuskegee, and numerous other private and denominational Negro colleges and academies, chiefly in the Southern states. Along with this has been the growth of state schools for Negroes, mostly normals, again in the South. Moreover, the Negro has had rather ready access to a good many of the outstanding colleges and universities of the North, such as Harvard, Columbia, Radcliffe, Wellesley, and others. Naturally this intellectual advancement has increased race consciousness and quickened in the Negro both desire and need for a literature of his own. The process has been gradual and not without early forecastings. By the end of the nineteenth century a representative Negro like Paul Laurence Dunbar had taken his place in American letters.

Nothing has been so characteristic of the development of a Negro literature as the evolution of Negro attitudes towards the folk-songs. James Weldon Johnson, in his "Preface" to *The Book of American Negro Spirituals,* says: "These songs passed through a period when the front rank of the Negro race would have been willing to let them die. Immediately following emancipation those ranks revolted against everything connected with slavery," and from slave quarters and slave life—the very flower of slavery—were the Spirituals. "It became a sign of not being progressive or educated to sing them." And then, referring to the newer attitude toward the same material, he continues, "The re-awakening of the Negro to the value and beauty of the spirituals was the beginning of an entirely new phase of race consciousness. It is a marked change in the attitude of the Negro himself toward his own art material." Discussing still further this new consciousness, this time the consciousness of the whites toward the Negro, Mr. Johnson continues: "America is beginning to see the Negro in a new light, or rather to see something new in the Negro. It is beginning to see in him the divine spark which may grow merely for the fanning. And so a colored man is soloist for the Boston Symphony Orchestra and the Philharmonic; a colored woman is soloist for the Philadelphia Symphony Orchestra and the Philharmonic; colored singers draw concert-goers of the highest class; Negro poets and writers find entrance to all the most important magazines;

Negro authors have their books accepted and put out by the leading publishers. And this change of attitude with regard to the Negro which is taking place is directly related to the Negro's change of attitude with regard to himself. It is new, and it is tremendously significant." It is thoroughly in keeping with the doctrine of selfhood advocated by American writers from Emerson and Whitman to the latest school of such authors and critics as Sherwood Anderson and Stuart P. Sherman.

A third aspect of the literary advance of the American Negro towards a place in the sun has to do with the changing attitude toward the whole subject of the Negro in American literature, either as a theme for literary expression by the whites or as participant himself in this literary expression. I find four rather obvious, if somewhat overlapping, aspects of this evolution during the period under discussion. The dates here given are only approximate, as are any other arbitrarily chosen dates to mark off periods or movements.

The first fifteen-year period (1865 to 1880) was devoted mostly to collecting Negro folk-lore, chiefly songs, merely as technical folk-lore. The second period of the evolution covers some thirty years, roughly from 1880 to 1910, and was marked by the transmutation of Negro folk-lore into literature of "local color." Merely to recall the work of such writers as Joel Chandler Harris, Thomas Nelson Page, and Francis Hopkinson Smith illustrates what I mean. The third period, a period interrupted, as all other literary movements were interrupted, by the World War, comprised the second decade of the present century, and was marked by a subjective consciousness which concerned itself with social and literary interpretations of Negro folk-lore. Of course, this advance was accompanied by an even greater diligence in gathering from hitherto ungleaned fields folk-lore of every kind. The fourth and last period, that of the half-spent present decade, is marked not only by the rise of the Negro himself to a high position as collector and interpreter of his own lore, but by the indisputably significant place he has attained as literary critic and as creative artist. Self-consciousness is evident sometimes, it is true; but in the language of "Daddy-Do-Funny's Jingles," by Ruth McEnery Stuart, the Negro

> Ain't by hisse'f in dat, in dat,
> He ain't by hisse'f in dat.

Indeed, America herself, as regards her literary advancement, is, and has been, even from before the time of her political independence, tremendously self-conscious.

These four periods in the literary emancipation of the Negro will be made more concrete by a bibliographical survey of Negro folk-lore. This survey is largely summarized from the bibliography appended to the valuable *The Negro and His Songs* by Howard W. Odum and Guy B. Johnson, of the University of North Carolina, supplemented by a section from "American Bibliography" for 1925, edited by Professor Norman Foerster and printed in the *Publications of The Modern Language Association of America*, Vol. XLI, No. 1, March, 1926. If such bibliography has the disadvantage of not being exhaustive, it has the compensating advantage of being selected by two of the foremost students of American Negro folk-lore. The items listed are, if not what might be called monumental, at least representative and highly significant. I shall not give them in detail but shall summarize them by decades since the first publication in 1867 to the last seven publications in 1925. The authors include the most prominent students of Negro folk-lore both white and black.

The table runs as follows:

The decade of the sixties, having one publication, *Slave Songs of The United States*, by W. F. Allen: words and music of 136 songs.

The decade of the seventies, comprising two publications:
  (a) *The Jubilee Singers*, by G. D. Pike: 61 religious songs.
  (b) *Hampton and Its Singers*, by M. F. Armstrong: 50 plantation songs.

The decade of the eighties, comprising two publications:
  (a) *Uncle Remus, His Songs and Sayings*, by Joel Chandler Harris.
  (b) *The Story of the Jubilee Singers*, by J. B. T. Marsh; an account of the Jubilee Singers with their songs.

The decade of the nineties, comprising two publications:
  (a) *Cabin and Plantation Songs*, by T. P. Fenner and F. G. Rathbun.

(b)   *Uncle Remus and His Friends,* by Joel Chandler Harris.

The first decade of the nineteenth century, comprising three publications:

(a)   *Creole Songs from New Orleans,* by C. G. Peterson.

(b)   *In Old Alabama,* by Anne Hobson: 10 dialect stories and songs.

(c)   *Religious Folk Songs of the American Negro,* by T. P. Fenner: words and music of 153 religious songs.

The second decade of the nineteenth century, comprising two publications:

(a)   *Afro-American Folk Songs,* by H. E. Krehbiel: careful study and collection of sixty or more songs.

(b)   *Folk-Songs of the American Negro,* by John Wesley Work: 55 songs and the music of 9 with a study of the origin of certain songs.

The first half of the present decade, comprising eight publications:

(a)   *The Black Border:* Gullah stories of the Carolina Coast, by Ambrose E. Gonzales: 43 stories of the Gullah dialect.

(b)   *Negro Folk Rhymes,* by Thomas W. Talley: about 350 rhymes and songs, together with a study of the origin, development, and characteristics of Negro rhymes.

(c)   *Black Cameos,* by R. Emmet Kennedy: a collection of twenty-eight stories, mostly humorous, with songs interwoven, and the words and music of seventeen songs.

(d)   *Folk-Songs of the South,* by J. H. Cox: a monumental collection of folk-songs, mostly by whites of the South, but incidentally throwing light on the origin of many Negro songs.

(e)   *The Negro and His Songs,* by H. W. Odum and G. B. Johnson: a critical discussion and literary analysis of 139 Negro songs of various kinds.

(f)   *On the Trail of Negro Folk-Songs,* by Dorothy Scarborough: some 200 songs of all kinds, together with informal discussion of methods of approach to folk-lore collection; valuable critical analysis of Negro folk-lore in general; music of 117 songs.

(g)   *Mellows: Negro Work Songs, Street Cries, and Spirituals,* by R. Emmet Kennedy: a discussion of adequately representative types indicated in the title.

(h)   *The Book of American Negro Spirituals,* by J. W. and J. Rosamond Johnson; illuminating "Preface" on the origin, nature, and literary and musical worth of the spirituals, together with the words and music of 55 spirituals set to music by J. Rosamond Johnson and Lawrence Brown.

An appended bibliography of twenty-four shorter studies, for the same general period, occurring in *The Journal of American Folk-Lore* and such magazines as *The Atlantic, The Century, The New Republic,* and *The Nation,* points to the same kind of activities and the same conclusions as are implied in the larger publications just cited. When it is remembered that of the twenty items in the larger bibliography, the authors who are of the white race found the co-operation of the Negro indispensable in their studies, and that a goodly number of the other studies are by prominent Negroes themselves, we are forced to recognize the advancement of the Negro as an interpreter of his own folk-lore.

Turning from quantity to quality, I wish to consider J. W. Johnson's *The Book of American Negro Spirituals* as a fact in the Negro's own literary emancipation. The book is both a study and a collection. The "Preface" is the criticism of an accomplished critic, and the rendition of the fifty-five spirituals into musical notation is the work of a gifted Negro composer. The soul and melody of the spirituals are here caught up into permanent form, preserving all the beauty that competent groups of Negroes or individual Negro singers, such as Paul Robeson or Roland Hayes, have realized in singing them.

The "Preface," as the most important study of its kind in the field of American Negro folk-lore, deserves special consideration. With unrestrained racial pride the author declares the spirituals to be "songs unsurpassed among the folk-songs of the world, and in the poignancy of their beauty unequalled. . . . America's only folk music." The source of their art he seems to find in the earnestness of the creators, and the failure of the white man to appreciate that art he ascribes to his lack of sympathy for the peculiar religious genius of the Negro. I can but agree with him. Often I have heard a chorus of a hundred or more Negroes, with faces bespeaking earnest, hungry souls, and with voices the melody and harmony of which evoked only the profoundest awe and the consciousness of beauty, lift their yearnings through the words of such songs as "Steal Away to Jesus," "Go Down, Moses," or "Deep River," until I have been transported to realms where only beautiful music can take me. And I have heard

white quartets sing these same songs with the effect of ex-
cruciating pain that only religious or artistic blasphemy can
give. "The capacity to feel these songs while singing them,"
says J. W. Johnson, "is more important than any amount of
mere artistic technique; to feel them, it is necessary to know
the truth about their origin and history, and to realize something of what they have meant in the experiences of the
people who created them."

Of course, the Negro took much of his imagery from the
Bible, and it may be that he derived something of music from
religious hymns sung by his white masters, but to quote
further from the "Preface" to *The Book of American Negro
Spirituals*, "the white people among whom the slaves lived
did not originate anything comparable even to the mere titles
of the spirituals." I must say that such titles as "I've
Got to Walk My Lonesome Valley," "Swing Low, Sweet
Chariot," and "Death's Going to Lay His Cold Icy Hand on
Me," like the titles of many of Walt Whitman's poems—
"Out of the Cradle Endessly Rocking," "I Hear America Singing"—seem indisputable evidence of a poetic mind of a high
order. The essential originality of the Negro is further seen,
as Johnson points out, in the Negro's creation of "America's
most popular medium of musical expression"—jazz.

But I cannot go on quoting forever from this prideful and
remarkable Negro interpretation of the Negro race's literary
genius. However, it is necessary to dwell somewhat on the
claims made for the spirituals as essential poetry. Conced-
ing crudeness, triteness, and irrelevant repetition, J. W. Johnson maintains that the spirituals yet have in them a sufficient
residue of beauty to give them a distinct place in the realm
of lyric poetry. The Hebraic paraphrases offer a peculiar
blend of Biblical imagery and racial psychology:

> I wrastled wid Satan and I wrastled wid sin
> Stepped over hell, and come back agin.
>
> Isaiah mounted on de wheel o' time,
> Spoke to God-A-Mighty way down de line.

A naive realism, blended with a crude pathos, is frequent:

> Dey crucified my Lawd,
> An' He nevah said a word.
> Dey crucified my Lawd,
> An' He nevah said a mumblin' word,
> Not a word—not a word—not a word.

I think a comparison with Wordsworth here is not out of place:

> But she is in her grave, and, oh,
> The difference to me!

But to continue with the crucifixion story, the Negro recites all the attendant circumstances of this great tragedy as conceived by his vivid imagination and expressed in accord with his spontaneous sympathy.   If he uses "twinklin' " instead of "trickling," his peculiar genius is no less striking:

> De blood come twinklin' down,
> And he nevah said a mumblin' word.
> De blood come twinklin' down,
> And he nevah said a mumblin' word—
> Not a word—not a word—not a word.

An occasional note of irrepressible humor comes out in such observations of the Negro as these:

> Ev'ybody talkin' 'bout heaben ain't goin' dar.
> Sister, you bettah min' how you walk on de cross,
> Yo' foot might slip an' yo' soul get los'.

But the note of intentional humor in the spirituals is rare. The Negro takes his religious experiences with a seriousness which is not surpassed by that of any other people.   Indeed, if one mood is more dominant in the spirituals than another, it is that of a weird and haunting pathos.   The note of spiritual loneliness holds the Negro to a melancholy seriousness that pervades by far the greater number of his religious hymns. Now and then in expressing this loneliness he hits upon the most fundamental human relationships:

> Sometimes I feel like a motherless child,
> Sometimes I feel like a motherless child,
> Sometimes I feel like a motherless child,
> A long ways from home.

Or the pathos may be tempered by pleasant anticipation of the joy to be attained in the far-away hereafter.   This particular blending of moods gives a peculiarly imaginative effect, especially when one realizes that there is in the Negro's imagery evidence of the singer's identity with the means by which he is to accomplish his heavenward flight:

> Sometimes I feel like an eagle in de air:
> Some o' dese mawnin's bright an' fair
> I'm goin' to lay down my heavy load;
> Goin' to spread my wings an' cleave the air.

The "eagle in the air" here may not be the patronizing, reassuring, and philosophical eagle that bore Dan Chaucer to the "House of Fame," but no doubt the Negro feels safer to be metamorphosed into the great bird himself than to be conveyed parachute fashion (an anachronism which would trouble neither Chaucer nor the Negro) for such an uncertain distance in the talons of a pagan bird like Chaucer's.

Quoting from a spiritual of which Colonel Thomas Wentworth Higginson was fond, Mr. Johnson concludes his study of the poetic qualities of the spirituals by saying: "Occasionally we are startled by a flash of poetry of pure beauty; of poetry not circumscribed by individual conditions, but coming out of the experiences of humanity":

> I know moon-rise, I know star-rise,
>   I lay dis body down.
> I walk in de moonlight, I walk in de starlight,
>   To lay dis body down.
> I walk in de graveyard, I walk throo de graveyard,
>   To lay dis body down;
> I lie in de grave an' stretch out my arms,
>   I lay dis body down.
> I go to de jedgment in de evenin' of de day
>   When I lay dis body down,
> An' my soul an' your soul will meet in de day
>   When I lay dis body down.

In order to get the full effect of the spirituals one must hear them in their proper setting; must look into the solemn, black faces of the singers; must feel the rhythm of their swaying bodies; must catch, though one can not hold or transcribe them, the harmonies and plaintive melodies fraught with the emotion and vivid imagination on which the Negro's soul reaches heavenward in search of the happiness that he feels will come some day when he is permitted to

Steal away, steal away to Jesus,
Steal away, steal away home.

I hope that I have now given some suggestion of the advance of the Negro as his own interpreter of folk-lore, and especially as an interpreter of the spirituals, which, in the words of the study that I have most quoted from, represent "the finest distinctive artistic contribution America has to offer the world."

SOUTH TEXAS NEGRO WORK-SONGS: COLLECTED AND UNCOLLECTED

BY GATES THOMAS

In treating of the Negro work-song I shall generally exclude both the spiritual and the controversial, or "shout," song, though all kinds of songs are sung by the Negro at work. The work-song I have in mind is a product of economic and labor conditions and, so far as I can observe, is found in its most authentic state among the "lusty, phallic, Adamic" Negroes of South Texas, shiftless and shifting day laborers and small croppers who follow Lady Luck, Aphrodite, and John Barleycorn. From just these unidealized Negroes have been gathered the work-songs that I wish to present, but before taking them up, it may be well to glance at what has already been done with the type.

The first significant anthology of Negro work-songs in this country was published by Dr. H. W. Odum, of the University of North Carolina, in the *Journal of American Folk-Lore,* XXIV, and enlarged into a volume, *The Negro and His Songs,* by Howard W. Odum and Guy B. Johnson, University of North Carolina Press, 1925. Hereafter when Dr. Odum's book is mentioned, Mr. Johnson's collaboration is implied. The book is a socio-psychological study of the casual Negro laborer east of the Mississippi, and as such it is more important than as a literary document. I understand that Dr. Odum contemplates issuing soon a volume to be made up exclusively of Negro work-songs with musical scores.

My impression is that both Dr. Odum and Miss Scarborough (in her *On the Trail of Negro Folk-Songs*), Harvard Press, 1925, have been handicapped by having to depend considerably on second-hand information, that is, on the auditory inaccuracies and interpretations of enthusiastic but not necessarily competent correspondents. It is, of course, possible that the Negroes whom these correspondents of Dr. Odum and Miss Scarborough heard sing all over the South are awkward in rhythm and inapt in words; I only know that the Fayette County and other South Texas "kinkies" whose songs I have been noting for nearly forty years are not so. Unprintable many of the songs may be, but pointless and unrhythmical they are not, as I trust my exhibit below will attest. The real problem of the Negro work-songs is not to find them, but to get them selected, classified, and expurgated for publication so that the point and quality of the songs are not impaired.

A noticeable folk-song need in Texas at present is for more music-writers of the proven competency and sympathy of Mr. R. E. Kennedy, who wrote *Mellows,* and of Miss Ola Lee Gulledge, who assisted Miss Scarborough in the book already referred to. Only by the help of such music-writers can the very important and interesting "indigoes," so protean in rhythmic and melodic arrangement, be set down in established rhythmic and melodic patterns. These songs called "indigoes" began appearing shortly before 1910. They nick in with the American poetic renascene of that time, and have some resemblance to the work of Sandburg and Millay. They make out-of-date some of the orthodox canons of ballad classification, in that they differ among themselves more in melody and rhythm than in subject matter and theme. The South Texas Negro laborer sings largely of work, wandering, and woman; sometimes he sings in lyric pattern, sometimes in narrative, often in a combination of lyric and narrative. Some tunes or melodies are comprehensive enough to include other tunes or melodies; as a result, the Negro can sing most of his songs to the same general melody. For instance, there is very little difference in melody between "The Boll-Weevil" and "Frankie and Albert."

I believe that my brother, Professor Will H. Thomas, of the Agricultural and Mechanical College of Texas, was one of the first, if not the first, of the Texas collectors to publish. In 1912 he included in his presidential address before the Texas Folk-Lore Society the words to a number of songs that we had collected together. The address was printed by the Society in pamphlet form and it received considerable notice, references and citations to the songs in it being found in such anthologies as Cox's *Folk-Songs of the South* (Harvard Press, 1925) and Gray's *Songs and Ballads of the Maine Lumber Jacks* (Harvard Press, 1925); several of the songs are reprinted in Miss Scarborough's *On the Trail of Negro Folk-Songs.* Although my brother and I have discovered a number of errors in his collection, space prevents including here amended versions. In *Publications* of the Texas Folk-Lore Society, Number II, Mr. W. P. Webb reported some negro songs from the Cuero district. Mr. John A. Lomax, aside from collecting cowboy songs, has collected Negro songs all over the state, but he has not published his collection, though he has drawn from it in lectures.

A great deal of Miss Scarborough's material is Texan, she having included in her book nearly everything available in printed form. Naturally in such a vast state with so few active collectors a great mass of songs remains untouched. My own contribution has been taken for the most part from Fayette and adjoining counties, a geographical area about thirty miles square, its center Winchester, its fringe including the towns of Bastrop, Smithville, Flatonia, La Grange, and Giddings. The Texas product collected and uncollected has its cognates and variants in anthologies by collectors of other states.

I have already spoken of Dr. Odum's important work, and shall have occasion to refer to it again. Thomas W. Talley's *Negro Folk-Rhymes* has versions of some of the songs to be treated. R. E. Kennedy's *Mellows* (A. and C. Boni, 1925) contains four work-songs, together with thirty-one spirituals and several street cries, and is certainly a faithful presentation of the Louisiana Negro's genius for song. The place of these songs is Gretna Green, across the river from New Orleans, the scene of the author's boyhood and of his present occupation as plantation owner. I only wish that Mr. Kennedy had included less of roseate reverie concerning the scenes of his childhood and more of the Negro's resonant and colorful "make-up" songs (songs made up and sung on the spot).

The Negro's normal method of building his songs makes classification of them difficult. I have them here in two general historical divisions:

I.   Those secured between 1886 and 1905.

II. Those secured since 1905.

Divisions I and II are further divided into three groups:

A.   Narratives.

B.   Songs in which the lyric element seems to predominate.

C. A miscellaneous group of recitatives or hurrah-songs.
After each song, I have put a date indicating approximately
when I found it. I have indicated what I know or conjecture
of each song's history or regional meaning, with such references to analogues or cognates as I have had time to work up.
Both notes and cross-references are incomplete. Titles of
the anthologies consulted follow:

J. H. Cox: *Folk-Songs of the South,* Harvard Press, 1925.

John A. Lomax: *Cowboy Songs,* Macmillan (Rev. Ed.), 1916.

R. E. Kennedy: *Mellows,* A. & C. Boni, 1925.

Odum, H. W., and Johnson, G. B.: *The Negro and His
Songs,* University of North Carolina Press, 1925.

Dorothy Scarborough: *On the Trail of Negro Folk-Songs,*
Harvard Press, 1925.

T. W. Talley: *Negro Folk Rhymes,* Macmillan, 1922.

I. SONGS SECURED 1887–1905
A. NARRATIVE

(1) DIDN'T HE RAMBLE

The man that butchered the ram,
  He butchered him for his life;
He sent to Cincinnati for
  A four-foot butcher knife.

Chorus:
Didn't he ramble! Didn't he ramble!
Oh, he rambled till the butcher cut him down!

The ram he had two horns,
    They reached up to the sky;
The eagle went up and built his nest:
    I heered the young ones cry.

The ram he had two horns,
    They reached up to the moon;
The butcher went up in January
    And didn't get back till June.

The hair on that ram's belly
    It reached to the ground;
The devil stole the finer strands
    To make his wife a gown.

The habits of that ram
    They hung upon the wall;
A couple o' gals came into the shop,
    Says, "We never eats mutton a-tall!"

Special Chorus:
Didn't they ramble! Didn't they ramble!
Oh, they rambled down the street and through the town!

There was a gal in our town,
    Her name was Sarah Clark;
She went to working at six o'clock,
    But didn't get through till dark.

Of all the animals in this world
    I'd ruther be a bull;
I'd curl my tail upon my back
    And graze[1] my belly full.

Of all the animals in this world
    I'd ruther be a boar;
I'd twist my tail into a knot
    And eat[1] forevermore.

Special Chorus:
    Wouldn't I get fat, etc.

Of all the animals in this world
    I'd ruther be a coon;
I'd clam way up some sycamore tree
    And grimace[1] at the moon.

---

[1]Of course, the Negro does not use these terms, except in the hearing of respectable people, but obscenities.

Wouldn't I grimace!   Wouldn't I grimace!
Oh, I'd grimace till the daylight drove me down!

And so on through a catalogue of animals, reptiles, and insects, to this characteristically farcical conclusion:

Oh, the man that owned the ram,
Well, he must-a been turribly rich;
But the man that made the song up
Wuz a lying son of a —————.

—1888.

I suppose that the foregoing song has a prototype or analogue in some of the frontier ballads; perhaps it is an improvement on the story of Dan Tucker.   The Negroes who gave it to me said its locale was a few miles up the Colorado River from La Grange, that the original ram was of the regulation "Darby" breed, and that he had developed the habit of knocking down pedestrians who came through his pasture, until a sagacious wood-cutter hung a "curly-ellum maul" from the limb of a live oak, against which the ram butted his head into such a state that his owner sold him to the butcher, who did eventually "cut him down" as aforesaid.

(2)   THE OLD HEN CACKLE

The old hen she cackle, she cackle in the corn;
The next time she cackle, she cackle in the barn.

Chorus:
Well, the old hen she cackle, she sholy gwain to lay.

The old hen she cackle, she cackle in the loft;
The next time she cackle, she cackle further off.

Chorus:
Well, the old hen she cackle, she sholy must-a laid.

The old hen she cackle, she cackle in the lot;
Well, the next time she cackle, she'll cackle in the pot.

Chorus:
The old hen she cackle, well, she sholy ought to lay.

—1886.

No. 2 is one of the liveliest dance tunes on the list, working into the organic melody the notes of the hen cackling. For analogues, see Talley, 50, 93.

Nos. 3–7 following I have arranged into a narrative sequence which I have termed *A Tragedy in Five Movements:*

(3)   THE DREAM

I dreamt last night I wuz walkin' aroun',
I met that Nigger and I knocked her down;

I knocked her down on the hop-joint floor;
Mr. Townsend[2] took at me wid his fo'ty-fo'.

I made a good run way up the track,
But they cotcht me on the Katy, an' he brings me back.

—1890.

(4)   NOBODY THERE[3]

That you, Nigger man, knockin' at my door?
Hear me tell you, Nigger man, "Nobody there no more."

—1890.

(5)   ONE MORNIN'

Got up one mornin', grabbed my gun,
Shot at my babe and started to run;

Started to run down the Katy track;
Mr. Loessin[4] got his Gatlin' for to bring me back;

Made a good run, but I runned too slow,
He landed me over in the Jericho;

He put me in the jail-house, I fell on my knees;
The first thing I noticed wuz a big pan o' peas;

---

[2] For some time a deputy sheriff at Smithville; now sheriff of Bastrop County, I think.

[3] A favorite expression equivalent to "useless," "preposterous," "unthinkable"; to our "nothing doing."

[4] Former sheriff of Fayette County; pronounced Lucine.

Well, the peas wuz hard and the bacon wuz fat,
But you ought'r seen the Niggers wuz grabbin' at that.

—1893.

(6) HUNTSVILLE-BOUN'

Last Saturday mornin' about the dawnin' of day,
The sheriff done come and arrested me, poor boy,
And 'livered me to the county jail.

Them jurymen foun' me guilty, the jedge he did say,
"This man's convicted to Huntsville, poor boy,
For ten long years to stay."

Black Mammy said, "It's a pity"; my luluh[5] said, "It's a shame;
They're takin' my man to Huntsville, poor boy,
For ten long years to stay."

Upon the deppo platform we all stood waitin' roun',
Waitin' for the train for Huntsville, poor boy,
Jest waitin' for the train to come down.

The train run into the deppo, the sheriff he did say,
"Get on this train for Huntsville, poor boy,
For ten long years to stay."

Now if you see my luluh, please tell her for me,
I've done quit drinkin' and gamblin', poor boy,
And gettin' on my sprees.

—1895.

Both songs 5 and 6 were included in the collection by W. H. Thomas and are also in the Scarborough collection.

(7) BEEN IN THE PEN SO LONG

---

[5]Luluh, sometimes a proper name, in the songs is generally a synonym for "honey," "woman," etc. "Black Mammy" here refers to one of his "women."

Been in the pen so long, been in the pen so long,
Been in the pen, Lord, I got to go again,
Been in the pen so long.

Don't like no Fort Worth gal; don't like no Fort Worth gal;
She'll meet you on the street and it's, "Baby, can't you treat?"
Don't like no Fort Worth gal.

But I like my Houston babe, I like my Houston babe;
She'll pat you on the head and it's, "Baby, go to bed;"
I like my Houston babe.

Well, Baby, your house rent's due, Baby, your house rent's due;
Just put on your bustle and make a little rustle,
And bring in a dollar or two.

But it's light out, you ———— ————, light out, you ———— ————:
You've fooled me again and I'm boun' for the pen;
So it's light out, you ———— ————.

—1890.

B. LYRICAL

Songs 8–12 below form a group of lyrics that have the common characteristic of having been sung by the "rounder" on his favorite theme—woman and lust.

(8)   DON'T LOVE-A NOBODY (Version A)

Chorus:
Oh, Lordy, oh, Lordy,
Don't love-a nobody.

I'm so glad the hogs all dead,
'Cause Niggers gwain to have a little cracklin' bread.

Chorus (in parts or ensemble, by the men):

A. My baby loves pork and greens.
B. My baby loves candy.

C. My baby likes whiskey straight.
D. My baby likes brandy.

Great big Nigger layin' in the bed,
Heels popped open like crack-er-lin' bread.

Chorus (by the women):

A. My baby's a salty dog.
B. My baby's a dandy.
C. My baby's a vinegar pup.
D. My baby's the candy.

Two little Nigger babies layin' in the bed,
One turned over, and the tother one said,

Chorus (ensemble or solus):

"You've wet in my warm place,
Gwain tel my mammy;
You've wet in my warm place,
Gwain tel your mammy."

I've been a-gettin' there, you've been tryin',
I've got a woman on the 'Ransas line.

I've been a-gettin' there, you've been a-tryin',
I've got a baby on the 'Ransas line.[6]

Chorus (women):
A. My baby lives down the slough.
B. My baby lives handy.
C. My baby's named Lishus U.
D. My baby's named Sandy.

Three, four, seven, two makes nine;
Luluh had a baby and she said it wuz mine.

Chorus (the rounder solus):

Black Mama had a ba-a-by;
Damn thing a-went cra-a-zy.
It's head was na-a-ppy;
I wa'n't its pa-a-ppy.

—1892.

---

[6]The San Antonio & Aransas Pass Railway, Waco Branch; now a part of the Southern Pacific lines.

Miss Scarborough devotes several pages (149–153) to variants of this song, classifying it as a lullaby, which it may have been in other parts of the country, just as, elsewhere, "crackling bread" may have been "a kind of bread made very rich by having bacon gravy and bits of crisp bacon mixed in it." As the reader has perhaps already inferred, this is a break-down song something like a square-dance in which there is opportunity for individual, group and *ensemble* participation.

Variant B below I secured from a Negro cook in Sherman, who was a fairly good self-taught musician and did a little adapting of his own, playing his results on an organ. I am sure variant B (9) shows effects of adaptation, as do "The Little Ball of Yarn" and "Baldy," to which I can only refer, as their pornography is such an organic part of their structure that it cannot be excised without destroying the point of the songs. All three songs are widely distributed over Texas and, perhaps, the South.

(9)   DON'T LOVE-A NOBODY (Version B)

Luluh, Luluh, were you mine, Babe,
You shouldn't do nothin' but wash and ine, Babe;
Wash and ine, Babe, cook and sew, Babe;
God bless yo' soul, Babe, you shouldn't do no mo', Babe.

Chorus:
Don't love-a nobody, nobody loves me,
'Ceptin-a my luluh; my luluh's stuck on me.

Luluh, Luluh, were you mine, Babe,
I'd take you a-ridin' on the I.&G.N. line, Babe;
The I.&G.N. line, Babe, runs so fast, Babe,
It sho' beats ridin' on the 'Ransas Pass, Babe.

Chorus:
My luluh loves candy, my luluh drinks tea;
My luluh is even[7] made, my luluh suits me.

Early in the mornin', sun did rise, Babe,
Lookin' in my luluh's eyes, Babe;
Late in the evenin', sun done set, Babe,
Ain't done lookin' at my luluh yet, Babe.

---

[7]That is, "symmetrical." The term is also used as an intensive.

Chorus:

Corn whiskey won't hurt you;
   'Twon't do you no harm;
Corn whiskey won't hurt you;
   It'll keep your baby warm.

Luluh, Luluh, let's to bed, Babe;
I'll lay my Gatlin' at my head, Babe;
I grease my Gatlin' with hog-eye lard, Babe;
I does all my creepin' in the white folks' yard.

Chorus:

Don't drink-a no toddy, don't drink-a no tea;
When I drink whiskey, my luluh drinks with me.

—1893.

(10) MY LULUH

You go ride the big bay horse,
I'll go ride the roan;
If you get there before I do,
Just let my luluh 'lone, Nigger man,
Just let my luluh 'lone.

White man goes to college,
Nigger to the field;
White man learns to read and write;
Poor Nigger learns to steal, Honey Babe,
Poor Nigger learns to steal.

Peaches in the summer time, apples in the fall;
Thought I heard my luluh say she wouldn't take none at all, Nigger man,
She wouldn't take none at all.

Beauty is only skin-deep, ugly to the bone;
Beauty quickly fades away, but ugly holds his own;
Honey Babe, ole ugly holds his own.

If you don't quit monkeyin' with my luluh, tell you what I'll do:
I'll feel aroun' your heart with my razor, and I'll cut you half in two,
Nigger man, I'll cut you half in two.

Train runned into Palestine sixteen coaches long;
Took all the money I had to put my luluh on,
Nigger man, to put my luluh on.

Engineer blowed the whistle, fireman rung the bell,
Conductor hollered "All aboard." Well, it wuz, "Luluh, fare you well,
　　Honey Babe,"
It wuz, "Luluh, fare you well."

Luluh went to Kansas, I tole her not to go;
Well, now the ole thing is in Kansas a-hustlin' in the cole ice and snow,
　　Honey Babe,
A-hustlin' in the cole ice and snow.

　　　　　　　　　　　　　　　　　　　　　　—1895.

(11)　I AIN'T BOTHERED

Said the ole rooster to the hen, "You ain't laid an aig in God knows
　　when."
Said the ole hen to the rooster, "You don't call aroun' any more, like
　　you use'ter."

Refrain
But I ain't bothered; no, I ain't bothered. [8]

Said the ole rooster with a bow, "Lots o' young hens learnin' how."
Said the ole hen with a twitch, "Nobody there, you proud son of a ——."

I went down to the house about six o'clock, tapt on the door and the
　　door was locked;
I jumped back and scratched my chin, for the coon can gambler wuz-a
　　settin' in
My rockin' cheer, my rockin' cheer.

I got a wife and a woman still; if my wife don't do right my woman
　　will;
And so, ole Nigger, you ought to be like me; instead o' one woman,
　　get you two or　three.
And you ain't bothered; no, you ain't bothered.

Well, they call me a rounder if I stay in town, and they say I'm a rounder
　　if I roam aroun';
I got it writ on the tail of my shirt: "I'm a nachel-bo'n rounder and
　　don't need to work."
And so I ain't bothered; no, I ain't bothered.

　　　　　　　　　　　　　　　　　　　　　　—1905.

For analogues of "I Ain't Bothered," see Odum, pages 176,
179, 211.

----

[8]The rhythm and melody here pretty well represent the insinuatingly amorous gurgle of the rooster in the earlier stages of his gallantry. The song is the most modern in this group and represents the Negro's re-synthesis of a pornographic bar-room ballad that was current (usually on the cards of whiskey-drummers) about the turn of the century.

Songs 12–17, inclusive, are associated with teaming and railroading, especially as these activities were conducted about the turn of the century. Analogues to all the songs but Number 17 in this group may be found in Scarborough and in Odum. Song 12 was brought into Fayette County by returned wanderers from Colorado and Wharton counties, where "jerk line" driving was used in managing teams of more than four mules, the driver usually riding the "near" tongue mule and using a jerk line and calling out "haw" and "gee" to direct the leaders and swingers. The unmindful mule in the song was perhaps a swinger that cut in too quickly or not quickly enough, and was "whopt" on the head for his waywardness.

(12)   GO ON, MULE, YOU BETTER STOP SADDLIN'

Hollered at the mule and the mule wouldn't mind;
Well, I whopt him in the head with the leadin' line,
And it's, "Go on, mule, you better stop saddlin'."[9]

Hollered at the mule and the mule wouldn't gee;
Well, I tuck him in the head with the singletree,
And it's, "Go on, mule, you better stop saddlin'."

(13)   DON' LET YO' WATCH RUN DOWN

Chorus:
Don' let yo' watch run down, Cap'n;
Don' let yo' watch run down.

---

[9]Prancing or dog-trotting in such a way as not to "get into the collar" on the swinging pulls.

Workin' on the levee,[10] dollar and a half a day,
Workin' for my luluh, gettin' mo' than pay, Cap'n,
Gettin' mo' than pay.

Chorus:
So don' let yo' watch run down, Cap'n,
Don' let yo' watch run down.

Workin' on the railroad, mud up to my knees,
Workin' for my luluh. She's a hard ole gal to please, Cap'n,
She's a hard ole gal to please.

When you see me comin' haist yo' windo's high;
When you see me leavin' hang down yo' heads and cry, brownskins,
Hang down yo' heads and cry.

—1892.

Song 14 represents the same teamster on Saturday or Sunday, the enthusiastic adjurer of "Lady Luck."

(14)   ROLL ON, JOHNNIE!

Chorus:
Oh, roll on, Johnnie; you rolls too slow;
For you roll like a man never rolled befo'.

I'm a man this-a way, gonna have my fun;
If a man don't like it, got to use his gun.

A railroad man ain't got no home;
He's here today, tomorrow he's gone.

I asked that boss-man[11] for to gimme my time;
Sez he, "Ole Nigger, you're a day behin'."

I asked him once, I asked him twaist;
Ef I ask him again, I'll take his life.

Ef I had money, like diamon's and gol',
I'd work today, then work no mo'.

—1891.

The singer has drawn, by at least a day's wage, more money

---

[10]Not necessarily the actual levee, but any earthen dump the Negro was engaged
in throwing up. Hence "levee-camp" is any construction camp.

[11]The Negro skinner makes a distinction between his Cap'n, or employer, and that
worthy's "straw-boss," or time-keeper, the latter being held as a negligible underling
above him in social status alone.

than he has earned; hence, if he quit, he would quit without money and in debt. Instead of putting the blame for this condition where it belongs—on his own unthrift or on the canniness of the "Cap'n"—he lodges it against the time-keeper. Compare the song with Odum, pages 252, 255.

(15) MY OLE MAN'S A RAILROAD MAN

My ole man's a railroad man, he works on Number Nine;
Gets his fifty dollars a month, and half that money's mine.

My ole man's a railroad man, he works on Number Four;
He's a rustlin' son of a ———, and I'm his dirty ———.

—1891.

(16) EAT WHEN YO'RE HONGRY

Chorus:
Eat when yo're hongry, drink when yo're dry,
An' ef a tree don't fall on you, you'll live tel you die.

The horses wuz mounted, the races wuz run;
Them ladies from Baltimo' came for the fun.

Oh, ladies, young ladies, don't think it unkin'
Ef I set down aside you and tell you my min'.

My min' is to marry a woman I knows,
Who will patch on my jumpers and make all my clo'es;

Who will wash 'em and ine 'em, and scrub up the flo',
An' keep the house tidy an' sweep 'roun' the do';

Who will cook up my vittuls and bake up my do',
And make down my pallet to lie on the flo'.

We'll eat when we're hongry and drink when we're dry,
And ef a tree don' fall on us, we'll live tel we die.

Songs 16 and 17 I submit as examples of domestic lyrics, which Dr. Odum implies (pages 160, 166) are rather scarce among the modern generation, for several reasons, the main one, to me, being the muting effect of the economic struggle. Song 16 seems to be a re-synthesis of "Rye Whiskey" and a variant of "The Noble Skewball."[12] Song 17 is, so far as I know, original.

---

[12]Scarborough, 61-64. See also Lomax, 292, and Talley, 114.

(17) ROLL THE BABY OUT

Get yo' little wagon, roll the baby out,
  Let him have a little fresh air;
Feed him on bananas, he'll never have the gout;
  Put yaller ribbons in his hair.

—1894.

C. RECITATIVES, HURRAH-SONGS

(18) A. GINGER BLUE

I'm A. Ginger Blue[13] and I tell you mighty true,
  I'm just from the Tennessee mountains,
Where the grass grows short and life is as sweet
  As the water that flows from their fountains.

One night Peter Williams wuz a-gwain to give a dance
  For us Niggers what live in the quarter;
Sez he, "A. Ginger Blue, I want you to come,
  And you may square my daughter."

No sooner he spoke the word, I wuz up, and like a bird,
A big ole consequated Nigger.
"Ole Nigger, ef I ketch you monkeyin' around my gal,
I'll make you walk-talk, A. Ginger Blue,
Get over double trouble, and hop on Virginia triumph."

—1890.

(19) TOM TWISS (Fragment)

Tom Twiss wuz a wonderful feller;
  His bones wuz so limber and strong,
He could turn ten somersets backwards
  And stand on his head all day long.

The intervening stanzas, which I have forgotten, explain
how his mother took such a pride in her offspring that he

---

[13]Name of a well-known race-horse, I am told, but have not been able to verify
the statement.

became her mainstay of social entertainment and came to
his end in "demonstrating" before guests:

> "Oh, very willingly, mother";
> So he with a skip and a hop
> He turned them somersets backwards
> But then wuz unable to stop.
>
> —1892.

(20) BILLY GELEF (Fragment)

> In come a man was tall and fat,
> He had on a Studson hat,
> Said his name was Billy Gelef,
> He had got so bad he wuz skeered of hisself.
>
> —1892.

The remaining stanzas of the song, forgotten, recount a
"coon can" game in which Billy is at first a spectator and
later a participating hero.

Song 21 seems to have a wide distribution[14] and to contain
the materials of legend. Aunt Dinah is represented as an
old crone, a sly toper with the Ananias technique of conceal-
ment. The song is really an impressionistic monologue interpreting the high points in an old-time country doctor's visit
to Aunt Dinah, a charity patient, whose "mizry," legend says,
was "wind-colic" induced by too much "gritted bread"—
spoon or pone bread made of grated nearly glazed field corn—
or too many near-ripe sweet potatoes eaten raw. The dots
within the lines represent the monologuist's mimetic repre-
sentation of the pathognomonics of her "mizry," her grunts
and groans in making the prescription doubly sure.

(21) OLE AUNT DINAH

Ole Aunt Dinah . . . sick . . . in .. the . . bed,
Sont for the doctor . . . . . . Doctor . . . said,
"Git up, Dinah . . . You ain't sick;
All you need is a hickory stick."

Ole Aunt Dinah . . . . layin' . . in the . . bed,
Looked at the doctor . . . . then . . . she said . . .
"I-a . . . has . . a . . . . great mizry, I knows . . . I's sick . . .
Gimme some whiskey, doctor, quick . . . . . !"

—1892.

---

[14]Talley, 53; Scarborough, 187-188.

It is to be presumed that Aunt Dinah, like Babe the Blue Ox in a similar case to be read of in James Stevens' *Paul Bunyan,* made a speedy recovery.

Songs 22 and 23 are typical of the hurrah song, in that the Negro sings them or talks them in making his brags at any social gathering.

(22)   BABY, TAKE A LOOK AT ME

Chorus:
Ho, lo, Baby, take a look at me.

Went to the hop-point, went in a lope;
Sign on the 'scription case, "NO MORE DOPE."

Old Crow Whiskey, Devil's Island Gin;
Doctor said it would kill him, but didn't tell him when.

Down to the river and back again,
Had a little money, but I blowed it in.

(23)   HOLLA DING

Chorus:
Holla ding,[15] and it ain't no lie,
I'm a-goin' to holla ding tel I die.

Got my gun, goin' to hol' it on a level,
And I ain't gonna stop tel I kill a nigger devil;
Got my pistol in my han'
And I ain't gonna stop tel I kill a Nigger man.

Nought's a nought, figger's a figger,
Figger for the white man, nought for the nigger.
Nigger and a white man playin' seven up,
Nigger won the money but was feard to pick it up.

Talk about one thing, talk about another;
But ef you talk about me, I'm gwain to talk about your mother.
Talk about these and you talk about those,
Well, ef you talk about me, I'm gwain to talk under yo' clothes.

Drink my coffee, drink my tea,
Then you walk about the country and you talk about me.
Hands in my pocket, head's on the wall,
I'll take a chaw terbaccer and I'll rounse[16] you all.

---

[15]I have never been able to ascertain the exact meaning of this phrase. Talley (270) says that "Holly Dink." a variant, is meaningless.

[16]*Rounse* means "out-talk," "out-repartee." The chance is that the Negro got the word from the German *garaus* and turned it to his own particular use.

Holla ding, well, it's holla ding;
Sez, I'll bet my money on any little thing;
Holla ding, an' it tain't no lie,
Well, I'm a-gonna holla ding tel I die.

—1891.

Songs 22 and 23 are both well-distributed throughout the South, and are often confused. See Odum, 179, 193, 218; Scarborough, 277.

II. SONGS SINCE 1905

A. NARRATIVES

Of the ballads and narratives since 1905, the most significant are "The Boll Weevil" and "Frankie and Albert," both of which I learned about 1907; they may be sung to the same air, one version of which I am giving below. The songs have had a wide circulation, appearing in one form or another in various collections. I give my version of only the first mentioned.

(24) THE BOLL-WEEVIL

Have you heard the lates', the lates' all yo' own,
It's all about them weevils gonna make yo' fa'm their home.
Gonna make it their home, Babe, gonna make it their home.

The boll-weevil says to the sharp-shooter,[17] "Pardner, let us go,
And when we strike that cotton patch, we'll take it row by row;
For it's our home, Babe, for it's our home."

_____

[17]A small insect like a midge, contemporary with the weevil and once thought as harmful.

The first time I seen him he wuz settin' on a square;
Well, the next time I seen him he wuz a-crawlin' everywhere,
Just a-huntin' him a home, Babe, just a-huntin' him a home.

The boll-weevil sez to the farmer, "I ain't bothered a bit;
So when you plant that cotton, be sure you plant it thick;[18]
For it's my home, Babe, for it's my home."

The sharp-shooter sez to the boll-weevil, "You ain't treatin' me fair;
For since I seen you last time, you've scattered everywhere.
Done found you a home, Babe, done found you a home."

The farmer sez to his ole wife, "We are in a terrible fix:
Foolin' with the weevils gonna keep us in the sticks,[19]
Without a home, Babe, without a home."

The ole wife sez to her husban', "I done my level bes'
Workin' with them weevils, and I ain't got but one dress.
It's full of holes, Babe, it's full of holes."

The farmer sez to his ole wife, "Well, what do you think of that?
I found a little boll-weevil right in my Sunday hat;
Done found him a home, Babe, done found him a home."

The farmer said to the merchant, "It is the general talk;
The boll-weevil's et all the cotton, and left us leaves and stalk.
We've got no home, Babe, we've got no home."

The merchant sez to the farmer, "What do you think of that?
Ef you ketch all them boll-weevils, make you present of a Stetson hat.
You'll have a home then, you'll have a home."

The boll-weevil sez to the sharp-shooter, "Pardner, what of that?
They say ef the farmer ketches us, gwain to give him a Stetson hat.
He'll have a time, Babe, he'll have a time."

So they took the little boll-weevil and they put him on the ice.
He sez to the farmers, "I say, but ain't this nice!
But it ain't my home, though; no, it ain't my home."

Then they took the little boll-weevil and buried him in hot sand.
He sez to the farmers, "Well, and I'll stand it like a man,
Though it ain't my home, Babe; no, it ain't my home."

---

[18]The bulk of experimentation now points to thick-planting as one of the cultural methods to beat the weevil instead of as a harborage as formerly regarded.

[19]The postoaks or the wooded upland small valleys, as distinguished from the mesquite flats and creek and river bottoms, where the farmer had a better chance at the weevil because of the opportunity to fire its hibernation quarters as well as use cultural methods. The native to these regions will find many other autochthonous touches in the poem.

The farmer said to the merchant, "I didn't make but one bale,
But befo' I'd bring that bale in, I'd fight you and go to jail;
For I've got to have a home, Babe, I've got to have a home!"

The boll-weevil sez to the farmer, "What make yo' neck so red?"
"Tryin' to beat you devils; it's a wonder I ain't dead;
For you're takin' my home, Babe, just a-takin' my home!"

"Well ef you want to kill us, I'll sho-God tell yo' how:
Just bundle up yo' cotton sack and th'ow away yo' plow;
Then hunt yo' a home, Babe, then hunt yo' a home."

—1906.

Fortunately, the calamity implied in the closing stanza has been more than averted, thanks to the application of scientific findings to cotton-growing and to the practical and creative work of such seed breeders as Mebane, Saunders, Ferguson, Bennett, Kasch, and others; but the ballad is still imaginatively true to the time and region in which it arose communally, from 1897, when I first heard stanzas 2, 3, 4 of the version above, to early in 1906, when I was given the song practically as above, by one of a group of Negro singers; another of the group, about a year later, gave me the MS of "Frankie and Albert," which was being synthesized in the same way about the same time.

All the singers from whom I got these songs read and write, taking some pride in writing them out for me. They have, however, a good deal of difficulty with their punctuation, words, and sentence structure. As a result, the collector has to do a good deal of interpreting and comparing and has to know the tunes. Often a Negro will write the verses to one tune and sing them to another, without recognizing his error. See Scarborough, 78, for an apparent mistaking by the transcriber of the Negro's meaning, as no Negro would say the boll-weevil had a red head.

B. Lyrics

(25) THIS MO'NIN', THIS EVENIN', SOMETIME

What you gwain to do when the meat gives out, my Baby?
What you gwain to do when the meat gives out, my Honey?
What you gwain to do when the meat gives out?
Gwain to set 'roun' my do' with my mouf in a pout,
    For sometime.

I'll be blamed ef I can see, my Baby,
I'll be blamed ef I can see, my Honey,
I'll be blamed ef I can see
How all my money got away from me.

What kin' o' pants does the gambler wear, this mo'nin'?
What kin' o' pants does the gambler wear, this evenin'?
What kin' o' pants does the gambler wear?
Big-legged stripes cost nine a pair
        This mo'nin'.

What kin' o' shoes does the gambler wear, this mo'nin'?
What kin' o' shoes does the gambler wear, this evenin'?
What kin' o' shoes does the gambler wear?
Yaller toothpicks, cost 'leven a pair
        This evenin'.

Slats in the bed went blam-to-blam, this mo'nin';
Slats in the bed went blam-to-blam, this evenin';
Slats in the bed went blam-to-blam;
Kep' on a-sleepin' like I didn't give a damn
        For sometime.

'Druther be dead an' in my grabe, this mo'nin';
'Druther be dead an' in my grabe, this evenin';
'Druther be dead an' in my grabe
Than to see somebody in the bed with my babe
        Sometime.

Who been here since I been gone, this mo'nin'?
Who been here since I been gone, this evenin'?
Who been here since I been gone?
Coon can gambler with a Studson on
        Sometime.

'Tain't no need in raisin' sand, this mo'nin';
'Tain't no need in raisin' sand, this evenin';
'Tain't no need in raisin' sand,
'Cause I got my Gatlin' in my han'
    This evenin'.

Standin' on a corner, didn't mean any harm, this mo'nin';
Standin' on a corner, didn't mean any harm, this evenin';
Standin' on a corner, didn't mean any harm;
Policeman grabbed me by my arm
    This evenin'!

Tol' that policeman to turn me loose, this mo'nin';
Tol' that policeman to turn me loose, this evenin';
Tol' that policeman to turn me loose.
Well, he turned me loose in the calaboose
    For sometime.

—1906.

(26) ALABAMA BOUN'

Chorus:
Alabama boun', Alabama boun',[20]
Ef you don' see me 'roun' here, Babe, I'm Alabama boun'.

Preacher in the pulpit jumpin' up and down,
While amen-corner sisters shout, "I'm Alabama boun'!"

Elder Green a-shootin' craps, and his point wuz ten.
Sez he, "I'm gwain to Waco now, for to try again,
For to try again, for to try again";
Sez he, "I'm boun' for Waco now, for to shoot again."

Elder Green is long-gone now, got a cross-tie pass;
He lef' here walkin' with his long coat on, on the 'Ransas Pass,
On the 'Ransas Pass, on the 'Ransas Pass;
He lef' here walkin' with his long coat on, on the 'Ransas Pass.

Rooster in the hoss-lot struttin' proud an' high;
Hen upon the haystack says, "You've got to rise an' fly,
Got to rise and fly, got to rise an' fly;
Ef you wan' me to love you, Babe, you've got to rise an' fly."

Rounders, when my times comes, bury me in black;
 So ef they meddle with that woman o' mine, I'll come a-sneakin' back,
Come a-sneakin' back, come a-sneakin' back;
Ef they meddle with that brown-skin o' mine, I'll come a-sneakin' back.

---

[20]A psychic state, rather than a place.

(27) ALICE BROWN

Rooster's a-crowin', day's a-breakin', sun's a-showin' his beams;
Wake up, sweet Alice, and tell me your midnight dreams.

Chorus:
Oh, Alice, oh, Alice, oh, Alice Brown,
Will you tell me now or wait tel after while?

Get your bonnet and your bucket; let's go to the wood.
And if you don't go now, you'll never do yo' man no good.

Chorus:
Oh, Alice, oh, Alice, oh, Alice Brown,
Do you want to now, or will you wait tel after while?

Lord, Alice, Lord, Alice, don't you trifle 'roun',
For I kain't come home tel this dirty-muddy water backs down.

Chorus:
No, Alice, no, Alice, no, Alice Brown,
Kain't come home, sweet Alice, tel this dirty-muddy water backs down.

—1914.

The "dirty-muddy" water in this instance is, presumably,
the big flood in the Colorado of December, 1913, as the lyric
was in process of synthesis about that time with a different
ending.

(28) YELLOW YAM PERTATERS

Last year wa'n't no very good year for cabbage and tomaters;
My pa didn't raise no cotton or corn, my pa didn't raise no cotton or
  corn,
My pa didn't raise no cotton or corn,
But, great God, yam pertaters!

Sal don't wear no button-up shoes, Sal don't wear no gaiters;
All Sal wants is a bottle of snuff *(Repeat twice for chorus)*
And yellow yam pertaters.

When the chilluns plays in Sal's back yard, she don't say nothin' about it;
Well, she ain't no hand to raise a row *(Repeat twice)*
But she's hell when she gets started.

I'm gwain to town to get a load of bricks, gwain to build my chimney
  higher,
To keep my neighbor's ole black cat *(Repeat twice)*
From puttin' out my fi-er.

Old missis had a big bulldog, they say he wuz double-jinted;
She took him to the blacksmith shop *(Repeat twice)*
To have his eye-teeth pinted.

—1915.

Hints and snatches of Number 28 may be had in Scarborough, 187, and in Talley, 46, 57.

(29) C. C. RIDER

C. C. Rider,[21] just see what you have done!
You made me love you, now yo' woman's done come!
You made me love you, now yo' woman's done come!

You caused me, Rider, to hang my head and cry;
You put me down; God knows, I don't see why!
You put me down; God knows, I don't see why!

Now it ain't no need, C. Rider, of your raisin' sand.
I'm a-gwain' to San 'Tonio, to see my soldier man.
I'm a-gwain' to San 'Tonio, to see my soldier man.

My home's on the water, I don't love land no mo';
I'll take him with me ef my soldier man wants to go;
I'll take him with me ef my soldier man wants to go.

I don't want no gravy, C. Rider, poured on my rice.
I just want my soldier man here to treat me nice.
I don't want no gravy, C. Rider, poured on my rice

C. HURRAH-SONGS, RECITATIVES

(30) THE BULLIN' MR. STAVIN' CHAIN

Now Stavin' Chain is dead and gone,
But he lef' me here to carry his business on.

Chorus:
Well, you kain't make it down
Like the bullin' Mr. Stavin' Chain.

Now Stavin' Chain wuz a man just so:
When he got good whiskey, he would gurgle it slow.

—1920.

---

[21] Who C. C. Rider was is to me unknown.

Song 31, which came to me first from a returned member of an overseas labor battalion and contains other stanzas, not printable, is a good example of an imaginative synthesis of the bull-roaring leader of a work-gang who was both "wo'kin' podemus" and rounder, as recited by an admiring follower. The narrator is presumed to be exploiting some of his own adventures as a wildcat.

(31)   UNCLE BUD

Well, when I asked that woman for to love me some,
She said I better wait tel Uncle Bud come.

Chorus:
Uncle Bud, Uncle Bud, what yo' doin', Uncle Bud?
Now, who in the hell is Uncle Bud?

Uncle Bud, Uncle Bud, he's a man in full,
And he's got habits like a Jersey bull.

Well, the scaredest I ever wuz in my life,
Uncle Bud kotch me lovin'-up his young wife.

—1925.

In conclusion, for making musical transcriptions used in this article, I wish to thank Miss Ola Gulledge, of San Antonio, Miss Mamie Sue Holbrook, of San Marcos, and Miss Lottie Holloway, of Hondo.

PROCEEDINGS OF THE ELEVENTH ANNUAL MEETING (1925) OF THE TEXAS FOLK-LORE SOCIETY

The Society met the afternoon and evening of May 9, 1925, in the Y.M.C.A. Auditorium of the University of Texas at Austin.
The programs as announced were as follows:

Afternoon

President's Address: *Some Legends of the Big Bend Country*, Mr. Victor J. Smith, Sul Ross State Teachers' College, Alpine.

Unseen Forces in the Battle of San Jacinto, Mrs. A. B. Looscan, Houston.

The Legend of the San Marcos and *The Legend of Tehuacana*, Mrs. Lillie Terrell Shaver, Dallas.

The Legend of Fort Phantom Hill, Mrs. Mamie Wynne Cox, Dallas.

The First Texas Legend, Miss Fannie Ratchford, the University of Texas.

Folk-Lore Helping Fiction: Some Recent Examples, Dr. R. A. Law, University of Texas.

Pictographs and Petroglyphs of the El Paso District, Colonel M. L. Crimmins, Fort Bliss.

Pictographs Near Paint Rock, Texas, Mr. O. L. Sims, Paint Rock.

Folk-Tales of the Kiowa Indians, Miss Laura V. Hamner, Amarillo.

Old-Time Darkey Plantation Songs, Mrs. Natalie Taylor Carlisle, Houston.

A Review of Professor John H. Cox's Folk-Songs of the South, Harvard Press, 1925, Dr. L. W. Payne, Jr., University of Texas.

Folk-Lore of Williamson County, Miss Martha Emmons, Taylor.

Business meeting: Election of officers, etc.

Evening

Hunting Treasure Down the Nueces and Out on the Pecos, Mr. J. Frank Dobie, Oklahoma Agricultural and Mechanical College, Stillwater, Okla.

Treasure Legends of Shoal Creek, Austin, Dean T. U. Taylor, University of Texas.

The Little Tree of Mount Bonnell and *The Crying Woman of the Rio Grande,* Miss Louise von Blittersdorf, Austin.

A Legendary Spanish Fort on the San Marcos and Its Treasure, Miss Bessie League, Austin.

Mrs. Looscan's paper, in her absence, was read by the Secretary; Colonel Crimmins was unable to attend but sent a large collection of pictographs for inspection. Miss Hamner and Mrs. Cox were absent and their papers were read by title.

Officers for the ensuing year were elected as follows:
President, Professor R. C. Harrison, Texas Technological College, Lubbock.
Vice-Presidents, Miss Adina de Zavala, San Antonio; Mrs. Mamie Wynne Cox, Dallas; Mrs. A. B. Looscan, Houston.
Councillors, Mr. Victor J. Smith, Alpine; Dr. L. W. Payne, Jr., University of Texas, Austin; Miss Julia Estill, Fredericksburg.
Recording Secretary and Treasurer, Miss Fannie Ratchford, University of Texas, Austin.
Secretary and Editor, Mr. J. Frank Dobie, University of Texas, Austin.
Miss Ethel Burch, retiring as Corresponding Secretary and Treasurer, was commended for her work in marketing *Legends of Texas,* a second edition of 1,500 copies having been printed; the first edition was of 1,250 copies. Miss Burch was voted $150 as partial compensation for her work. The financial report was accepted as it is recorded in the minutes.

The Texas State Historical Association met on May 8, thus allowing several persons from out of town to attend in one trip its meeting and also that of the Texas Folk-Lore Society.

CONTRIBUTORS

Mary Jourdan Atkinson until a few weeks ago was just "Miss Mary." Three years ago she was editor of *The Longhorn*, the University of Texas literary magazine. She comes of pioneer Texas stock and can "speak the language" of her people.

Edwin R. Bogusch is of German extraction, has lived in Bexar County most of his life, and is intimately qualified to continue the faithful work he has been doing for the Texas Folk-Lore Society.

Douglas Branch is the author of *The Cowboy and Cowboy Literature* to be issued soon by D. Appleton and Company. He is a Houstonian, but for the past three years has been studying history in the universities of Iowa and Ohio. He wrote his Master's thesis on cowboys and is writing his Doctor's thesis on the buffalo.

Mrs. Natalie Taylor Carlisle, a prominent woman of Houston, has for years been an ardent worker for the Texas Folk-Lore Society, of which she has been Councillor. Her father was N. A. Taylor, author of *The Coming Empire or Two Thousand Miles in Texas on Horseback* (1877), one of the very best travel books that Texas can claim. From it "The Devil and Strap Buckner" was reprinted in *Legends of Texas* (1924).

R. C. Harrison is Professor of English and head of the department in Texas Technological College, Lubbock. For 1925–1926 he was President of the Texas Folk-Lore Society.

Mrs. Mattie Austin Hatcher, Archivist in the University of Texas, is a thorough scholar of the Spanish period in Texas history, in which she has done much research work. She is descended from a cousin of Stephen F. Austin's.

Branch Isbell drove up the old Chisholm Trail from Texas to Kansas in the seventies. His account of early day experiences in *Trail Drivers of Texas* (republished by Lamar and Barton, Dallas, 1925) is one of the best things in that extraordinary source book. He has as much life now as when he danced the Virginia reel, ran the tournament, and put the *mangana* (roped by the forefeet) on Texas longhorns down the Nueces more than half a century past. His post office is McKinney, Texas.

Mrs. Mary Daggett Lake of Fort Worth is descended from one of the best known families of the Texas cattle business, the Daggetts. She has written a monograph on the Texas blue bonnet, frequently contributes feature articles to newspapers, and is compiling a history of Tarrant County.

Dr. L. W. Payne, Jr. has annually made his appearance in the *Publications* of the Texas Folk-Lore Society. He has a refreshing gusto for Texas folk-songs and is anxious to collect more of them. As Professor of English in the University of Texas he bears the reputation of being a humanist—which means a good deal more than being merely human.

John K. Strecker, Librarian of Baylor University, contributed an interesting "snake story" to the *Publications* of this Society last year. He is engaged in writing a book on the reptiles of the Southwest.

Gates Thomas, President of the Texas Folk-Lore Society for 1926–1927, is Professor of English and head of the department in the Southwest Texas State Teachers' College at San Marcos. His father used to entertain Sam Houston on the Thomas plantation below La Grange, and thereby hangs another good Sam Houston anecdote. Would a collection of anecdotes of which Sam Houston is the hero come within the province of folk-lore? Let E. G. Littlejohn, of Galveston, make reply and report.

INDEX

The purpose of this index is to afford convenient reference to the folk-lore of the Southwest. Bibliographical material such as that catalogued by Professor Harrison in his article and footnote references have not been indexed. Dr. Payne's article is itself so much a compendium of the names of informants and their regional associations that they have been omitted in the index.

WILL THOMAS AND THE TEXAS FOLK-LORE SOCIETY

Now that this brochure is being reprinted by the Texas Folk-Lore Society, I take the opportunity to say a word concerning its author and its history.

Although not a numbered publication, **Some Current Folk-Songs of the Negro** (1912) was the first item produced by the Texas Folk-Lore Society. At the time dues to the Society were two-bits a year—not enough to allow a very extensive publication. Number I (now reprinted under the title of **Round the Levee)** was not issued until 1916; then it was seven more years before another volume was issued, since which time, 1923, the Society has sent out a book annually to its members. The credit for initiating the Society's policy of recording the lore of Texas and the Southwest belongs to Will H. Thomas.

At the time his pamphlet was issued, he was president of the organization, to which office he was elected again in 1923. His idea was that people who work with folk-lore should not only collect it but interpret it and also enjoy it. This view is expressed in his delightful essay on "The Decline and Decadence of Folk Metaphor," in **Publications** Number II (**Coffee in the Gourd**) of the Society.

The view is thoroughly representative of the man, for Will Thomas was a vigorous, sane man with a vigorous, sane mind. He had a sense of humor and, therefore, a sense of the fitness of things. For nearly thirty years he taught English in the Agricultural and Mechanical College of Texas, and I have often wished that more professors of English in the colleges and universities over the country saw into the shams and futilities and sheer nonsense that passes for "scholarship" as thoroughly as he saw into them. Yet he was tolerant. He was a salt-of-the-earth kind of man.

He was born of the best of old-time Texas stock on a farm in Fayette County, January 11, 1880; he got his collegiate training at Austin College, Sherman, and the University of Texas and then took his Master's degree at Columbia University. He was co-editor, with Stewart Morgan, of two volumes of essays designed for collegians. He died March 1, 1935. Gates Thomas, Professor of English in Southwestern State Teachers College at San Marcos, who has done notable work in Negro folk songs and who is one of the nestors and pillars of the Texas Folk-Lore Society, is his brother.

J. FRANK DOBIE
Austin, Texas
April, 1936

SOME CURRENT FOLK-SONGS OF THE NEGRO AND THEIR ECONOMIC INTERPRETATION.

BY W. H. THOMAS, COLLEGE STATION, TEXAS.

Mr. President, Members of the Folk-Lore Society, Ladies and Gentlemen:

I should first like to say a word as to why I have been given the honor of addressing this meeting. Mr. Lomax is solely to blame for that. A short while after this society was organized, Mr. Lomax approached me one day while I was holding an examination and asked me to join the society and to make a study of the negro songs. He did so, no doubt, out of a knowledge of the fact that as I had lived all by life in a part of the State where the negroes are thick, and as I was then devoting my summers to active farming where negroes were employed, I would, therefore, have an excellent opportunity for studying the negro and his songs, as the geologist would say, *in situ.*

You will notice that I have taken as my title, "Some Current Folk-Songs of the Negro and Their Economic Interpretation." Now it is somewhat misleading at this day and time to speak of the negro as a "folk." That word seems to me to be applicable only to a people living in an industry in which economic function has not been specialized. So it would be more accurate to speak of "negro class lore." The class that I am treating of is the semi-rural proletariat. So far as my observation goes, the property-holding negro never sings. You see, property lends respectability, and respectability is too great a burden for any literature to bear, even our own. Although we generally think of beliefs, customs, and practices, when we hear the word "folk-lore" used, I believe all treatises on the subject recognize songs, sayings, ballads, and arts of all kinds as proper divisions of the subject. So a collection and study of the following songs is certainly not out of place on a program got up by this society.

Now just one word more under this head. I have found it very difficult to keep separate and distinct the study of folk-lore and the study of folk-psychology. The latter has always been ex-

tremely interesting to me; hence I can't refrain from sharing with
you the two following instances: A negro girl was once attend-
ing a protracted meeting when she "got religion" and went off
into a deep swoon, which lasted for two whole days, no food or
drink being taken in the meantime. A negro explained to me as
follows: "Now when that nigger comes to, if she's been possumin', she sho' will be hungry; but if she hasn't been possumin',
it will be just the same as if she had been eatin' all the time."
The other instance is that of an old negro who just before he died
had been lucky enough to join a burial association which guar-
anteed to its members a relatively elaborate interment. So, when
this old negro died, the undertaker dressed him out in a nice
black suit, patent leather shoes, laundered shirt and collar, and
all that. His daughter, in relating the incident after the funeral,
said: "Bless your life, when they put Pappy in that coffin, he
looked so fine that he just *had* to open his eyes and look at his
self."

I imagine that folk-lore appeals differently to different individ-
uals according to what intellectual or cultural interest predominates
their beings. I suppose that the first interest in folk-lore was
that of the antiquarian. Then came the interest of the linguist
and the literateur. But it seems to me that if the pursuit of
folk-lore is to be thoroughly worth while to-day the interest must
above all be psychological and sociological. At least these are my
interests in the subject. For instance, take that piece of well
known folk-lore—the belief that by hanging a dead snake on a
barbed wire fence—one can induce rain in a time of drought. I
would give almost anything to know just how the two ideas "hanging a snake on a fence" and "raining" were ever associated. But
I can perhaps still better illustrate my attitude by relating a piece
of Herbert Spencerian lore. Herbert Spencer tells in his autobi-
ography of this incident that he met with while on one of his
annual trips to Scotland. The house at which he was a guest
contained a room which bore the reputation of being haunted. It
was in this room that Herbert Spencer was asked to sleep. So he
did and lay awake most of the night, though not out of fear that the
ghost would choose that particular night to pay a visit, but out of
a philosophical curiosity to figure out the origin of such a "fool"
belief.

In reference to these songs, when I say that I am interested in a study of origins, I do not mean the origin of any particular song, but the origin of the songs as a social phenomenon. Or to put it interrogatively, why do the members of this particular class sing, and why do their songs contain the thoughts that they do?

I believe it is pretty generally agreed today that any well-defined period of literature is merely the reflection of some great economic change. I notice that the critics have begun to speak of Victorian literature as merely the ornament of nineteeth century prosperity—the prosperity that was incident to the utilization of steam as motive power.

Now a great change has come into the negro's economic life within the past two decades. Its causes have been two. He has come into competition with the European immigrant, whose staying qualities are much greater than his; and agriculture has been changing from a feudalistic to a capitalistic basis, which requires a greater technical ability than the negro possesses. The result is that he is being steadily pushed into the less inviting and less secure occupations. To go into the intricacies of my thesis would be to abuse the privilege of the program; so I shall have to content myself with merely stating it. The negro, then, sings because he is losing his economic foothold. This economic insecurity has interfered most seriously with those two primal necessities—work and love—and you will notice that the thoughts in all these songs cluster around these two ideas.

So much for the interpretation; now for the appreciation. It has been my experience that where a knowledge of the negro's every day, or rather every-night, life is lacking, the appreciation of these songs is never very keen. Hence, in order to make it certain that you will appreciate these songs, I deem it necessary to try to acquaint you with the life of one of the "songsters." Otherwise I am afraid that too many of you will look upon these songs as absolutely puerile. Remember that a greater man than you or I once declared the ancient ballads to be without merit and also maintained that he could write, on the spur of the moment, a stanza that was just as good and that contained just as much meaning. Whereupon, being challenged he sat down and wrote:

"I put my hat upon my head and went into the Strand,
And there I met another man with his hat in his hand."

The colored semi-rural proletárian, then—how shall I describe him so that you may see him in your mind's eye, as I read these songs? I don't know how many of you are already acquainted with him, but, if any of you have ever tried to employ him profitably, I am sure you will never forget him. Perhaps I can picture him best by using the method of contrast. Let us follow one as he works with a white man, the latter, of course, being boss. We shall start with the morning.

The white man rises early and eats his breakfast. My proletarian doesn't rise at all for the chances are that he has never gone to bed. At noon they "knock off." While the white man is preparing to eat his lunch, the "nigger" has already done so and is up in the bed of a wagon or on a plank underneath a tree fast asleep, usually with his head in the sun. At nightfall, the white man eats supper and spends the evening reading or with his family. Not so my proletarian. He generally borrows thirty-five cents from the white man, steps out the back gate, gives a shrill whistle or two, and allows how he believes he'll "step off a piece to-night."

As I have not been on the farm much for the last two years. I have been unable to use the Boswellian method of recording these songs but have had to depend mostly on memory. The result is that some of them are not complete and some may not be textually correct. Of course the collection is not anything like an exhaustive one.

If you consider these songs as the negro's literature, you will notice some striking parallels between its history and that of English literature. As all of you know, English literature for several centuries was little more than paraphrases of various parts of the Bible. The first songs I shall read you are clearly not indigenous but are merely revamping the Biblical incidents and reflections of the sect disputes of the whites. The first song here presented is one that I heard twenty years ago as it was sung on the banks of a creek at a "big baptizing." It is entitled:

TELL ALL THE MEMBERS I'M A NEW BORN.

I went to the valley on a cloudy day.
O good Lord!
My soul got so happy that I couldn't get away.

Chorus.

Tell all the members I'm a new-born,
I'm a new-born, I'm a new-born,
O Lord!
I'm a new-born baby, born in the manger,
Tell all the members I'm a new-born.

Read the Scriptures, I am told,
Read about the garment Achan stole.

Chorus.

Away over yonder in the harvest fields,
O good Lord!
Angels working with the chariot wheels.

Chorus.

Away over yonder, got nothing to do,
O good Lord!
But to walk about Heaven and shout Halloo.

Chorus.

I'm so glad, I don't know what about,
O good Lord!
Sprinkling and pourings done played out.

Chorus.

Here are two more of the same kind:

PREACHING IN THE WILDERNESS.

Daniel in that lion's den,
He called God A'mighty for to be his friend;
Read a little further, 'bout the latter clause:
The angel locked them lions' jaws.

Refrain.

Oh, Daniel, hallelujah;
Oh, Daniel, preaching in that wilderness.

Old man Adam, never been out;
Devil get in him, he'll jump up and shout;
He'll shout till he give a poor sister a blow,
Then he'll stop right still and he'll shout no more.

Refrain.

P's for peter; in his word
He tells us all not to judge;
Read a little further and you'll find it there,
I knows the tree by the fruit it bear.

Refrain.

SAVE ME FROM SINKING DOWN.

Seven stars in his right hand,
  Save me from sinking down.
All stars move at his command,
  Save me from sinking down.

Refrain.

Oh, my Lord, save me from sinking down.

John was a Baptist, so am I,
  Save me from sinking down.
And he heard poor Israel's cry,
  Save us from sinking down.

The following is only a snatch, but it is enough to show that the economic factor was not yet predominant. In it we still see traces of the Bible's influence:

O Lord, sinner, you got to die,
  It may be to-day or to-morrow.
You can't tell the minute or the hour,
  But, sinner, you've got to die.
          Refrain.

We now come to songs originated by the present generation of negroes. They all deal with work and love. The following might be entitled:

THE SONG OF THE FORTUNATE ONE.

The reason why I don't work so hard,
I got a gal in the white folks' yard;
And every night about half past eight,
I steps in through the white man's gate;
And she brings the butter, and the bread, and the lard;
That's the reason why I don't work so hard.

The next I have termed the "Skinner's Song." Skinner is the vernacular for teamster. The negro seldom carries a watch, but still uses the sun as a chronometer; a watch perhaps would be too suggestive of regularity. Picture to yourself several negroes working on a levee as teamsters. About five o'clock you would hear this:

I lookt at the sun and the sun lookt high;
I lookt at the Cap'n and he wunk his eye;
And he wunk his eye, and he wunk his eye,
I lookt at the Cap'n and he wunk his eye.

I lookt at the sun and the sun lookt red;
I lookt at the Cap'n and he turned his head;
And he turned his head, and he turned his head,
I lookt at the Cap'n and he turned his head.

The negro occasionally practices introspection. When he does, you are likely to hear something like this:

White folks are all time bragging,
  Lord, Lord, Lord,
'Bout a nigger ain't nothing but waggin,
  Lord, Lord, Lord.

Or,

White folks goes to college; niggers to the field;
White folks learn to read and write; niggers learn to steal.

Or,

Beauty's skin deep, but ugly's to the bone.
Beauty soon fades, but ugly holds its own.

The following is the only song in which I think I detect insincerity. Now the negro may have periods of despondency, but I have never been able to detect them.

THE RAILROAD BLUES.

I got the blues, but I haven't got the fare,
I got the blues, but I haven't got the fare,
  I got the blues, but I am too damn'd mean to cry.

Some folks say the rolling blues ain't bad;
Well, it must not 'a' been the blues my baby had.

Oh! where was you when the rolling mill burned down?
On the levee camp about fifteen miles from town

My mother's dead, my sister's gone astray,
And that is why this poor boy is here to-day.

If any of you have high ideas about the universal sacredness of domestic ties, prepare to shed them now. It has often been said that the negro is a backward race. But this is not true. In fact, he is very forward. He had invented trial marriage before sociology was a science.

The following songs are only too realistic:

FIRST.

I dreamt last night I was walking around,
I met that nigger and I knocked her down;
I knocked her down and I started to run,
Till the sheriff done stopped me with his Gatling gun.

I made a good run, but I run too slow,
He landed me over in the Jericho;
I started to run off down the track,
But they put me on the train and brought me back.

SECOND.

Says, when I die,
  Bury me in black,
For if you love that of woman of mine,
  I'll come a sneakin' back;
For if you love that woman of mine,
  I'll come a sneakin' back.

THIRD.

If you don't quit monkeying with my Lulu,
  I'll tell you what I'll do;
I'll fling around your heart with my razor;
  I'll shoot you through and through.

That the negro's esthetic nature may be improving is indicated by the following song. For tremendousness of comparison, I know nothing to equal it. It is entitled:

THE BROWN-SKINNED WOMAN.

A brown-skinned woman and she's chocolate to the bone.
A brown-skinned woman and she smells like toilet soap.
A black-skinned woman and she smells like a billy goat.
A brown-skinned woman makes a freight train slip and slide.
A brown-skinned woman makes an engine stop and blow.
A brown-skinned woman makes a bulldog break his chain.
A brown-skinned woman makes a preacher lay his Bible down.
I married a woman; she was even tailor made.

You will find plenty of economics in the following song. The present-day negro early made that most fatal of all discoveries: namely, that a man can really live in this world without working. Hence his *beau ideal* is the gambler, and his *bête noir* is the county jail or the penitentiary.

THE GAMBLER'S PANTS.

What kind of pants does a gambler wear?
Great big stripes, cost nine a pair.

JACK O' DIAMONDS.

Jack o' Diamonds, Jack o' Diamonds,
Jack o' Diamonds is a hard card to roll,

Says, whenever I gets in jail,
Jack o' Diamonds goes my bail;
And I never, Lord, I never,
Lord, I never was so hard up before.

You may work me in the winter,
You may work me in the fall;
I'll get e-ven, I'll get e-ven,
I'll get even through that long summer's day.

Jack o' Diamonds took my money,
And the piker got my clothes;
And I ne-e-ver, and I ne-e-ver,
Lord, I never was so hard run before.

Says, whenever I gets in jail,
I'se got a Cap'n goes my bail;
And a Lu-u-la, and a Lu-u-la,
And a Lulu that's a hard-working chile.

TO HUNTSVILLE.

The jurymen found me guilty, the judge he did say:
  "This man's convicted to Huntsville, poor boy,
For ten long years to stay.

My mammy said, "It's a pity." My woman she did say:
  "They're taking my man to Huntsville, poor boy,
For ten long years to stay."

Upon that station platform we all stood waiting that day,
  Awaiting that train for Huntsville, poor boy,
For ten long years to stay.

The train ran into the station, the sheriff he did say:
  "Get on this train for Huntsville, poor boy,
For ten long years to stay."

Now, if you see my Lula, please tell her for me,
  I've done quit drinking and gambling, poor boy,
And getting on my sprees.

DON'T LET YOUR WATCH RUN DOWN, CAP'N.

Working on the section, dollar and a half a day,
  Working for my Lula; getting more than pay, Cap'n,
Getting more than pay.

Working on the railroad, mud up to my knees,
  Working for my Lula; she's a hard old girl to please, Cap'n,
She's a hard girl to please.
  So don't let your watch run down, Cap'n,
  Don't let your watch run down.

BABY, TAKE A LOOK AT ME.

I went to the jail house and fell on my knees,
The first thing I noticed was a big pan of peas.
The peas was hard and the bacon was fat;
Says, your oughter seen the niggers that was grabbin' at that.

Refrain.

Oh, Lord, Baby, take a look at me!

Brandy, whisky, Devil's Island gin,
Doctor said it would kill him, but he didn't tell him when.

Refrain.

Oh, Lord, Baby, take a look at me!

DON'T YOU LEAVE ME HERE.

Don't you leave me here, don't you leave me here,
For if you leave me here, babe, they'll arrest me sure.
They'll arrest me sure.
For if you leave me here, babe, they'll arrest me sure.

Don't leave me here, don't leave me here,
For if you leave me here, you'll leave a dime for beer.

Why don't you be like me, why don't you be like me?
Quit drinking whisky, babe, let the cocaine be.

It's a mean man that won't treat his woman right.

The following is a tragedy in nine acts:

FRANKIE.

Frankie was a good girl, as everybody knows,
She paid a hundred dollars for Albert a suit of clothes:
He was her man, babe, but she shot him down.

Frankie went to the bar-keeper's to get a bottle of beer;
She says to the bar-keeper:"Has my living babe been here?"
He was her man, babe, but he done her wrong.

The bar-keeper says to Frankie: "I ain't going to tell you no lie,
Albert passed 'long here walking about an hour ago with a nigger named
      Alkali."
He was her man, babe, but he done her wrong.

Frankie went to Albert's house; she didn't go for fun;
For, underneath her apron was a blue-barrel 41.
He was her man, babe, but he done her wrong.

When Frankie got to Albert's house, she didn't say a word,
But she cut down upon poor Albert just like he was a bird.
He was her man, babe, but she shot him down.

When Frankie left Albert's house, she lit out in a run,
For, underneath her apron was a smoking 41.
He was her man, babe, but he done her wrong.

"Roll me over, doctor, roll me over slow,
Cause, when you rolls me over, them bullets hurt me so;
I was her man, babe, but she shot me down."

Frankie went to the church house and fell upon her knees,
Crying "Lord 'a' mercy, won't you give my heart some ease?
He was my man, babe, but I shot him down."

Rubber-tired buggy, decorated hack,
They took him to the graveyard, but they couldn't bring him back.
He was her man, babe, but he done her wrong.

And, once more, the female of the species was more deadly than
the male.